Some Other Books by A. J. Liebling:

The Telephone Booth Indian
The Road Back to Paris
The Wayward Pressman
The Honest Rainmaker
The Sweet Science
Normandy Revisited

The Earl
of Louisiana

BY A. J. LIEBLING

SIMON AND SCHUSTER / NEW YORK / 1961

PUBLISHED BY SIMON AND SCHUSTER, INC.
ROCKEFELLER CENTER, 630 FIFTH AVENUE
NEW YORK 20, N.Y.

THIRD PRINTING

LIBRARY OF CONGRESS CATALOG CARD NUMBER: 61-7017

Much of the material in this book origi-
nally appeared in *The New Yorker*.

MANUFACTURED IN THE UNITED STATES OF AMERICA
BY AMERICAN BOOK—STRATFORD PRESS, INC.

CONTENTS

CHAPTER I

"JOE SIMS, WHERE THE HELL?"

Southern political personalities, like sweet corn, travel badly. They lose flavor with every hundred yards away from the patch. By the time they reach New York, they are like Golden Bantam that has been trucked up from Texas—stale and unprofitable. The consumer forgets that the corn tastes different where it grows. That, I suppose, is why for twenty-five years I underrated Huey Pierce Long. During the early thirties, as a feature writer for a New York evening paper, I interviewed him twice—once at the brand-new Waldorf and once at the brand-new Hotel New Yorker. The city desk showed what it thought of him by sending me instead of a regular political reporter; the idea was that he might say something funny but certainly nothing important. He said neither. Both times he received me in his pajamas, lying on top of his bed and scratching himself. It was a routine he had made nationally famous in 1930, when, as Governor of Louisiana, he so received the official call of the commander of

7

a German cruiser visiting New Orleans, causing the Weimar Republic to make diplomatic representations. New York reporters couldn't figure out how he expected to get space with the same gag every time he came to town, but now I think I understand. He was from a country that had not yet entered the era of mass communications. In Louisiana, a stump speaker still tells the same joke at every stop on a five-speech afternoon. He has a different audience each time, like an old vaudeville comic, and Huey just hadn't realized that when a gag gets national circulation it's spoiled.

It was the same with his few remarks intended to be serious. He would boast of free schoolbooks, which we had had in New York since before he was born, and good roads, which ditto. Then, talking in the shadow of the new Empire State Building, he would brag about the thirty-four-story Capitol he had built in Baton Rouge. As for the eight bodyguards he brought with him, they seemed in New York an absurd affectation: didn't he know we had cops? And who would bother to shoot him anyway? It is hard to put yourself across as a buffoon and a potential martyr at the same time, and Huey did not convince us in either role. A chubby man, he had ginger hair and tight skin that was the color of a sunburn coming on. It was an uneasy color combination, like an orange tie on a pink shirt. His face faintly suggested mumps, and he once tipped the theater-ticket girl in the lobby of the Hotel New Yorker three cents for getting him four tickets to a show that was sold out for a month in advance.

Late in July 1959 I was in Baton Rouge, and I took a taxi out to the Capitol, where he is buried. Standing by Huey's grave, I had him in a different perspective. A heroic, photographically literal statue of him stands on a high pedestal above his grave in the Capitol grounds. The face, impudent, porcine and juvenile, is turned toward the building he put up—all thirty-four stories of it—in slightly more than a year, mostly with Federal money. The bronze double-breasted jacket, tight over the plump belly, has already attained the dignity of a period costume, like Lincoln's frock coat. In bronze, Huey looks like all the waggish fellows from Asheville and Nashville, South Bend and Topeka, who used to fill our costlier speakeasies in the late twenties and early thirties. He looks like a golf-score-and-dirty-joke man, anxious for the good opinion of everybody he encounters. Seeing him there made me feel sad and old. A marble Pegasus carved in bas-relief below his feet bears a scroll that says, "Share Our Wealth." That was one of Huey's slogans; another was "Every Man a King."

I walked along well-tended paths between melancholy Southern trees to the entrance of the Capitol, which is reached by forty-eight granite steps, each bearing the name of a state, in order of admission to the Union; to include Alaska and Hawaii, Louisiana will have to raise the Capitol. My taxi driver, a tall prognathous type who was a small boy when Huey was killed, had parked his cab somewhere and now sociably rejoined me. "The newspapers gave old Huey hell when he built that for five mil-li-on," he said, waving toward the skyscraper. "You couldn't build it now for a hundred mil-li-on." He talked of Huey as a contemporary, the way some people in Springfield, Illinois, talk of Lincoln.

Inside the Capitol, which is air-cooled, I paused, breathless with gratitude. Outside, the heat was pushing a hundred. The interior of the building is faced with agate, porphyry, basalt, alabaster and such—more than thirty kinds of stone, the *Louisiana Guide* says. It is the richest thing in its line since they moved the barbershop in the Grand Central Station upstairs. The rotunda, as slick as mortuary slabs on end, reminded me pleasurably of Grant's and Napoleon's tombs, the shrines that early fixed my architectural tastes forever. Marble, high ceilings and a reverential hush are the things I like inside a public building—they spell class. In addition to all this, and air-conditioning, the Capitol has its legend, and perhaps its ghost, hurrying along the corridor at the rear of the first floor. Looking around, I thought of what the Chief Justice of the Supreme Court of Louisiana had told me a day earlier about how Huey was shot in this monument he had erected to himself.

At sixty-four the Chief Justice, the Honorable John Baptiste Fournet, is still a formidable figure of a man—tall and powerful and presenting what might be considered in another state the outward appearance of a highly successful bookmaker. The suit he had on when I saw him, of rich, snuff-colored silk, was cut with the virtuosity that only subtropical tailors expend on hot-weather clothing. Summer clothes in the North are makeshifts, like seasonal slipcovers on furniture, and look it. The Chief Justice wore a diamond the size of a Colossal ripe olive on the ring finger of his left hand and a triangle of flat diamonds as big as a trowel in his tie. His manner was imbued with a gracious warmth not commonly associated with the judiciary, and his voice reflected at a distance of three centuries the France from which his ancestors had migrated, although he pronounces his name

"Fournett." (The pronunciation of French proper names in Louisiana would make a good monograph. There was, for example, a state senator named DeBlieux who was called simply "W.") I had gone to the Chief Justice to talk politics, but somehow he had got around to telling me instead about the night of September 8, 1935, which has the same significance among Longites that St. Bartholomew's Day has for French Protestants.

Huey had come down from Washington, where he was serving as United States Senator, to run a special session of the Louisiana Legislature, Justice Fournet said. He controlled the state from Washington through a caretaker Governor named O. K. Allen, but whenever there was a bit of political hocus-pocus to be brought off that he thought was beyond Allen's limited competence, he would come home to put the legislators through their hoops himself. When Huey was in Baton Rouge, everybody called him Governor. Since he feared assassination, he had a flat furnished for him on the thirty-fourth floor of the Capitol, and theoretically he would retire to it at the end of each legislative day, but, Fournet said, "He was the kind of man who was always running around so they couldn't keep him in that apartment. He was a hard man to guard." Fournet himself had served as Speaker of the House—it was he who adjourned the Legislature when Huey's enemies were about to impeach him—and, after that, as Lieutenant Governor under Allen. Huey had later looked after his old friend by pushing his election as an Associate Justice of the State Supreme Court. The Court was in the front line of conflict, because, as the Chief Justice explained to me, "There was hardly a piece of legislation that Huey introduced that the other side didn't carry to litigation. Huey had what he called a 'deduct' system—ten per cent of the salary of every state employee for his political fund. It sounds raw, but he had to take the money where he could; the other side had all the money of Standard Oil to pay its attorneys. I was elected for a term of fourteen years, and on the day I took the oath of office I had to start thinking about my campaign for re-election." On September 8, 1935, the Chief Justice said, he had to see Huey personally about some friends who needed political help, so he drove up to Baton Rouge from New Orleans, where the Supreme Court sits, and arrived at the Capitol just before nine at night, when the Legislature was to recess. Here he offered a slight digression. "People from out of state sometimes ask me why the Supreme Court sits in New Orleans when the capital is Baton Rouge, only eighty miles away," he said. "I tell them the truth—that there wasn't a road you could count on until Huey got in office, so the busy lawyers of New Orleans would have spent half their lives traveling back and forth. Now you can make it in an hour and a half, thanks to Huey, but the Court has stayed in New Orleans, mostly from habit."

When Fournet reached the Capitol, Huey was in the House chamber, on the second floor, co-ordinating the efforts of his legislators, and Fournet walked in and took a seat. He had the Senator under his eye, but when the session broke, there were a number of people between them, and Huey started out the door so fast that Fournet couldn't get to him. "That man never walked," he told me. Huey headed toward the corridor in the rear of the building that led to Governor Allen's office, and Fournet followed, content to catch Huey when he came out after leaving a few instructions with the titular Governor of Louisiana. There were bodyguards in platoon strength in front of the Senator and behind him as he trotted. Entering the corridor, Fournet saw a couple of rich dilettante politicians who were always good for a campaign contribution. He stopped to talk to them and then went on. Huey had disappeared into Allen's office. Fournet, as he followed him, passed two or three men standing in a recess in the wall, talking. He paid them no heed, assuming that they had just emerged from the House chamber, as he had. Then Huey came out of Allen's door, turning, with the knob still in his hand, to shout an inquiry back into the room. Fournet heard the answer: "All of them have been notified, Governor." He started toward Huey, and as he did a young man came up on his right side and passed him, walking fast. What attracted the Justice's attention was that he had a stubby black pistol in his right hand. "It was a hot night—before air-conditioning —and I perspire exceptionally," Justice Fournet said. "So I was holding my Panama hat in my right hand while I wiped my head with a handkerchief in my left. Without thinking, I hit at the man with my hat, backhand. But he reached Huey and fired, and Murphy Roden, a bodyguard, grabbed his gun hand and got a finger inside the trigger guard, else he would have killed Murphy. Huey spun around, made one whoop, and ran down the hall like a hit deer. Murphy and the young man went to the floor, both holding that gun and Murphy trying to reach his own gun with his other hand. I was leaning over them, thinking to grab hold, and Elias Coleman, another guard, leaned, too, and fired two bullets that passed, by the mercy of God, between Murphy and me and killed the fellow.

He let go his gun and lay there. He had black hair, combed down a little slick, as I remember it, and black-rimmed eyeglasses. Huey ran clear to the end of the hall and down a flight of stairs. Then the other guards pulled the body over to the wall and emptied their guns into it. It sounded like machine guns."

When Huey got to the lower hall, a couple of fellows he knew stopped him. One said "Are you hit?" and he said "Yes." The other said "Are you hurt bad?" and Huey said "I don't know." They put him in their car and took him to the Our Lady of the Lake Hospital. There, the examining surgeon found that the bullet had perforated Huey's colon and part of one kidney. "I couldn't ride with Huey, because it was a two-seated car," the Chief Justice said, "so I went to get mine, parked not far away, and by the time I saw him again he was on the examining table at the hospital. He felt strong and didn't think he was going to die. 'I want you to be more charitable toward Wade Martin and Ellender,' he said." (Martin was the chairman of the Public Service Commission, and Allen Ellender is now the senior United States Senator from Louisiana.) "He knew that all three of us wanted to be Governor, but he wanted us to get along together." It reminded me of how an old friend of mine, Whitey Bimstein, described the death of Frankie Jerome, a boxer he was seconding in the Madison Square Garden ring. "He died in my arms, slipping punches," Whitey said. Huey, mortally shot, talked politics.

Alone, except for the taxi driver, in the rotunda of the Capitol, I thought I heard Huey make his one whoop, but the sound may have been a mere hallucination. In any case, I felt different about Huey when I walked out into the heat. By that time I had been in Louisiana about ten days, and I had also changed my mind about Earl Long, then Governor of the state. Earl was Huey's brother, his junior by two years and his survivor by a quarter of a century, and although Fournet had said that Earl "wouldn't make a patch on Huey's pants," it seemed to me that he was filling a pretty fair pair of country britches.

For one thing, the expression of conventional indignation is not so customary in Louisiana as farther north. The Louisianians, like Levantines, think it naïve. A pillar of the Baton Rouge economy, whom I shall here call Cousin Horace, had given me an illustration, from his own youth, of why this is so.

"When I was a young man, fresh out of Tulane," he said, "I was full of civic consciousness. I joined with a number of like-minded reformers to raise a fund to bribe the Legislature to impeach Huey. To insure that the movement had a broad popular base, subscriptions were limited to one thousand dollars. When I went to my father, who was rich as cream, to collect his ante, I couldn't get but five hundred from him—he said he felt kind of skeptical. So I put up a thousand for me and the other five hundred for him. I wouldn't pass up a chance to give the maximum for such a good cause.

"A vote of two-thirds of each house was needed to impeach, and there were then thirty-nine state senators. But before our chairman could see enough of them, Huey induced fifteen—a third plus two—to sign a round robin stating they would not impeach no matter *what* the evidence was. Earl

says now that he thought of that scheme. We were licked, so
I went around to the eminent reform attorney who was treasurer of our enterprise and asked for my money back.

" 'Son,' he said, 'I am keeping *all* the subscriptions as my
fee.'

"I was mad as hell, and told Dad, and he said, 'Son, it shows
I did right to hold out my other five hundred—I gave it to
Huey as part of the contribution he levied on me to pay the
fellows on *his* side.' "

Cousin Horace, who looks like Warren Gamaliel Harding,
the handsomest of Presidents, imbibed deeply of a Ramos
gin fizz.

"Right then," he said, after the interval, "I made up my
mind that it didn't make any difference which side was in in
Louisiana, and I have stuck to business ever since."

It was Cousin Horace who told me that the disparity between the two Longs was not one of shrewdness but of scope.
"Earl is just as smart a politician inside the state as Huey
was," he said, "but Huey saw things big.

"I'll give you an example. One evening during Prohibition,
Huey came around to my dad's house and said, 'Telemon, I
need a drink.' My father went down to his cellar—he prided
himself on it—and brought up a bottle of pre-World War
One Jack Daniel. When he started to open it Huey said,
'Don't open that bottle for me, Telemon; it's too good. I'll
take it.'

"So he put it in his pocket and left. Earl would have given
Dad a drink out of the bottle."

I had left New York thinking of Earl as a Peckerwood
Caligula. Dispatches in the New York papers had left small

doubt that he had gone off his rocker during the May session of the Legislature, and I wanted to see what happens to a state when its chief executive is in that sort of fix. The papers reported that he had cursed and hollered at the legislators, saying things that so embarrassed his wife, Miz Blanche, and his relatives that they had packed him off to Texas in a National Guard plane to get his brains repaired in an asylum.

By late July, when I arrived in Louisiana, he had heaved himself back into power by arguing his way out of the Texas sanitarium, touching base at a New Orleans private hospital and legalizing his way out of the Southeast Louisiana State Hospital, at Mandeville. Then he had departed on a long tour of recuperation at out-of-state Western race tracks that most of the lay public had never heard of before he hit them. Just after I disembarked from my plane in New Orleans I read in the local *Times-Picayune* that the "ailing Governor" had got as far back toward home as Hot Springs, Arkansas, a resort famous for reconditioning old prize fighters and race horses. He had promised to be back in the state on August 1, in time to begin stumping for renomination as Governor in the Democratic primary elections, four months away.

"You know, I think ol' Earl will just about do it again," the taxi driver said as we descended the Capitol's forty-eight states. The place had started him thinking about the Longs. "It don't set good how they done him like they done, y'un-nerstand. Those doctors. And his wife. Saying he was crazy. It'll be like the last time he run, in '56. Two days before the primary, you couldn't find nobody to say he was going to vote for him. Then they all voted for him. And two days later you couldn't find nobody would admit to have voted that way."

With the Governor unavailable, I sat down in New Orleans to await his return and meanwhile try to build up a frame of reference, as the boys in the quarterly magazines would say. Politics is to the conversation of Louisiana what horse racing is to England's. In London, anybody from the Queen to a dustman will talk horses; in Louisiana, anyone from a society woman to a bellhop will talk politics. Louisiana politics is of an intensity and complexity that are matched, in my experience, only in the republic of Lebanon. The balance between the Catholics in southern Louisiana and the Protestants in northern Louisiana is as delicate as that between the Moslems and the Christians in Lebanon and is respected by the same convention of balanced tickets. In Louisiana there is a substantial Negro vote—about a hundred and fifty thousand—that no candidate can afford to discourage privately or to solicit publicly. In the sister Arab republic, Moslem and Christian candidates alike need the Druse vote, although whoever gets it is suspected of revolutionary designs.

The grand gimmick of Louisiana politics, however, providing it with a central mechanism as fascinating as a roulette wheel, is the double-primary system for gubernatorial nominations. The first primary is open to anyone who can get up the registration fee of two hundred and ten dollars. This brings out as many entries as the Preakness or the Kentucky Derby. If any candidate has more than fifty per cent of the total votes, he wins the nomination, which means that he will automatically be elected, since Democratic nomination is a ticket to the Governor's Mansion. If no one has a clear majority, the two top men have a runoff in a second primary, held about a month later.

It is unusual for a candidate to win first time around, and if one does he arouses a certain amount of resentment as a spoilsport. After the first primary, each beaten candidate and his backers trade off their support to one of the two men who are still alive, in exchange for what he will bind himself to do for them in the way of legislation, patronage or simple commercial advantage. Naturally, the runoff candidate who looks more likely to win can buy support at lower political prices than the other fellow, but by trying to drive too hard a bargain he may send the business to the underdog. Many a man has beaten himself that way. A Louisiana politician can't afford to let his animosities carry him away, and still less his principles, although there is seldom difficulty in that department.

In the campaigning days before the first primary, topics of conversation are delightfully unlimited; the talkers guess at not only how many votes a candidate will get in the first primary but what he will trade them off for, and to whom, if he fails to make the second. It is like planning carom shots or four-horse parlays.

In 1959, the date for the first Louisiana primary was December 5, and in July conversation was already intense. The talk centered on Long and whether he would be able to get to the post. I found few people, even among Long's worst friends, who believed that he was "crazy," although there were some who said he had been at the time of his deportation. (This second position, however, was hard to defend in public discussion. "Crazy" and "not crazy," like "guilty" and "not guilty," are terms that, in popular usage, admit of no shading in between; being crazy or being not crazy is considered a permanent condition, like having one leg.) In New York, the stories of his conduct on his Western tour of convalescence may have seemed clear evidence that the old boy was mad—the phrenetic betting on horse races, the oddly assorted roadside purchases (forty-four cases of cantaloupes, seven hundred dollars' worth of cowboy boots, and such), the endless nocturnal telephone calls, the quarrels with his friends and guards—but seen from New Orleans they indicated a return to normal. Earl had always been like that, fellows who knew him said. A summary of his physical condition had been released to the press by the physicians who examined him after his discharge from the State Hospital at Mandeville on June 26. The doctors' workup on the Governor looked dreadful to a layman—bum ticker, series of cerebral accidents, hardening of the arteries, and a not otherwise described condition called bronchiectasis. But there were lay experts who said that it was all a fake—that no doctor had been able to lay a hand on Earl to examine him.

A Louisiana political tipster never expresses a reservation, and when politics extends over into the field of pathology the positiveness extends with it. "I know a fella that Earl carries with him all the time, hear? and he says Earl just playing mousy, y'unnerstand?" summed up one extreme position. The opposing view could be summarized as "I know a fella told me they gave him adrenalin right in his heart, hear? and that means the old alligator is in extremis, y'unnerstand?" On my first evening in New Orleans, I received forty-two other prognoses in between.

Nor was there any agreement on the efficacy of the device whereby Earl, in entering the primaries, was challenging the Louisiana constitution, which provides that a governor may not succeed himself directly. Earl, bowing to this law, had dropped out after his 1948–52 term, and then had returned in 1956. Now, however, he was raising the point that if he resigned before election—the formal, post-primary, election, that is—his Lieutenant Governor would become Governor, and so he, coming in to begin a new term, would be succeeding not himself but the fellow who had succeeded him. Even Huey had not thought of that one.

What I heard from Long men was that it was the way the law read that counted, hear? and not what the framers had wanted it to signify. From the other side I heard that there wasn't a court in the country but would hold against a little fine-print loophole, and yeah, you resigned, but, yeah, you can't get away with that. Another point of dispute was how near the Governor stood to Federal prison.

The Income Tax people were reportedly on his trail, and apparently they were not being as hermetically secretive as they are supposed to be, or else the Natty Bumppos stalking Earl had stepped on a couple of dry twigs. The range of the opinion on this point lay between "They got it on him this time, hear?" and "Uncle Earl is just too smart to get caught so easy. Whatever he got, he'll say it was campaign contributions, same as Nixon in '52. That's why he's got to keep on campaigning, y'unnerstand?" (There is no statutory limit on campaign contributions in the state of Louisiana, and Earl Long often said, like Brother Huey before him, that he was campaigning all the time.)

Arranged in capsule form, all the areas of disagreement about the Governor, peacefully soaking his hide in the Arkansas vats, came to this: The perfect sour-on-Long man held that he was likely to die before the primaries, sure to get licked if he survived, certain to be thrown out by the State Supreme Court if nominated, and bound to be in jail before he could be inaugurated. The perfect Long man expressed faith that the Governor was as full of fight as a man twenty years younger, that he would probably win the first primary with seventy per cent of the vote, that he had the Louisiana Supreme Court in his pocket, and that if campaign contributions weren't income for a Republican like Nixon, they weren't income for a Democrat like Uncle Earl.

On my first night in town, before I had finished my third Sazerac at the little bar in Arnaud's Restaurant while waiting for a table, I was not only indoctrinated but willing to bet. An outsider, I had no feedbox information and less idea of the form, but I had an analogy, and nothing can seem more impressive to a man drinking on an empty stomach.

"When Pat McCarran was seventy-one," I said to the pair of home experts with me, "he had a heart attack so bad that they were laying eight to one against him in the Nevada Turf Club, but he recovered and lived seven years to ruin every politician who hopped off him when he was sick. He was mean. How old is Uncle Earl?"

"Sixty-three," said one expert.

"Is he mean?"

"Mean as hell," said the other.

"You see?" I said. "It's a lock." It was an insight that wouldn't have come to me if Arnaud's had not been doing such a good business, but we got a table just in time to prevent my laying money.

When we had ordered moderately—crabmeat Arnaud, filet mignon *marchand de vin,* and a bottle of Smith-Haut-Lafitte '47—we got back to politics. One of my convives, a lawyer, said that the Governor had deep pockets lined with fishhooks: "When you're with him and he picks up a newspaper, you lay down the nickel." The other man, a newspaperman and former Nieman Fellow at Harvard named Tom Sancton, whom I had known for some time, maintained that old Earl wasn't so bad. "He gives money to every kid he meets," he said. " 'A quarter to whites and a nickel to niggers' is the way you hear it around here."

The "nickel to niggers" is a key to the Long family's position on the Southern issue. "They do not favor the Negro," a Negro educator once told me, "but they are less inflexibly antagonistic than the others."

"Earl is like Huey on Negroes," Tom said. "When the new Charity Hospital was built here, some Negro politicians came to Huey and said it was a shame there were no Negro nurses, when more than half the patients were colored. Huey said he'd fix it for them, but they wouldn't like his method. He went around to visit the hospital and pretended to be surprised when he found white nurses waiting on colored men. He blew high as a buzzard can fly, saying it wasn't fit for white women to be so humiliated. It was the most racist talk you ever heard, but the result was he got the white nurses out and the colored nurses in, and they've had the jobs ever since."

A Negro minister in Baton Rouge said to me, later: "Earl

is a politician—and a human being." The combination, he
evidently felt, was rare.

Since the Governor was not available in the flesh, my
friends took me after dinner to see and hear him on film. In
the projection room of television station WDSU, which is off
a handsome Creole courtyard in the French Quarter, they
had arranged for a showing of a documentary composed of
various television-newsreel shots, and from this encounter I
date my acquaintance with Uncle Earl. The cameramen had
covered all the great moments of that fulminating May session of the legislature, which began with the Governor riding
high and ended, for him, when he was led from the floor,
tired and incoherent, by Margaret Dixon, the managing
editor of the Baton Rouge *Advocate*.

A day later he was under heavy sedation and on his way to
Texas, where he arrived, he subsequently said, with "not
enough clothes on me to cover a red bug, and a week later
I was enjoying the same wardrobe." But within a fortnight
he had talked a Texas judge into letting him return to
Louisiana on his promise to matriculate at a private hospital
in New Orleans. After signing himself in and out of the New
Orleans hospital, the Governor had started for Baton Rouge
to assume power, only to be stopped by sheriff's deputies at
the behest of his wife, Miz Blanche, who had then committed
him to the State Hospital at Mandeville. Thence he had been
rescued by a faithful retainer, the lawyer Joe Arthur Sims,
who sought a writ of habeas corpus. Once the Governor had
regained temporary liberty, he completed the job by firing
the director of the Department of Hospitals and the superintendent of the hospital, who, in the normal course of events,

might have appeared against him to contend that he was insane.

In the opening newsreel shots Long appeared a full-faced, portly, peppery, white-haired man, as full of *hubris* as a dog of ticks in spring, sallying out on the floor of the Legislature to wrest the microphone from the hands of opposition speakers. "Let him talk, Governor, let him talk," a man in the foreground of the picture—perhaps the Speaker—kept saying during these episodes, but the Governor never would. He would shake his finger in his subjects' faces, or grab the lectern with both hands and wag his bottom from side to side. He interrupted one astonished fellow to ask, "What's your name?"

"John Waggoner, from Plain Dealing." (This is the name of a town.)

"Well, well, you look like a fine man. Don't let nothing run over you."

Some of the newsreel clips were of the Governor's press conferences, and in one, when a reporter asked him whether he thought he could manage his legislators, he said, "You know, the Bible says that before the end of time billy goats, tigers, rabbits and house cats are all going to sleep together. My gang looks like the Biblical proposition is here." This was the first good sample of his prose I had had a chance to evaluate, and I immediately put him on a level with my idol Colonel John R. Stingo, the Honest Rainmaker, who, at the age of eighty-five, is selling lots at Massena, New York, a community he predicts will be the Pittsburgh of the future.

In another remark to a reporter I thought I detected a clue to what was to set him off. The Governor said he had

reduced 29 pounds, from 203 to 174, in a few months at his
doctor's behest. To do this he must have been hopped up
with thyroid and Dexedrine, and his already notorious temper,
continually sharpened by ungratified appetite, had snapped
like a rubber band pulled too hard.

Khrushchev, too, looks like the kind of man his physicians
must continually try to diet, and historians will some day
correlate these sporadic deprivations, to which he submits
"for his own good," with his public tantrums. If there is to
be a world cataclysm, it will probably be set off by skim milk,
Melba toast, and mineral oil on the salad.

The newsreel also included a sequence in which the Governor sounded off on Mayor deLesseps S. Morrison of New
Orleans, who for years had been his rival in Democratic primaries. "I hate to say this—I hate to boost old Dellasoups—
but he'll be second again." (Long beat Morrison badly in the
1956 race for Governor. He always referred to him as "Dellasoups" and represented him as a city slicker.) "I'd rather
beat Morrison than eat any blackberry, huckleberry pie my
mama ever made. Oh, how I'm praying for that stump-
wormer to get in there. I want him to roll up them cuffs,
and get out that little old tuppy, and pull down them shades,
and make himself up. He's the easiest man to make a nut out
of I've ever seen in my life." The "tuppy," for "toupee,"
was a slur on Morrison's hair, which is thinning, though
only Long has ever accused him of wearing a wig. As for the
make-up, Morrison occasionally used it for television. Earl's
Morrison bit was a standard feature of his repertoire, and I
could see from the mobile old face how he enjoyed it. Morrison took the "dude" attacks so to heart that in his last cam-

paign he performed dressed like Marlon Brando in deshabille.

And, as if to illustrate the old Long vote-getting method, which had worked in Louisiana ever since Huey took the stump in 1924, the newsreel anthologist had included part of a speech of the Governor's, evidently favoring a higher license fee for heavy (rich men's) vehicles. "Don't you think the people that use the roads ought to pay for building them? Take a man out in the country, on an old-age pension. He don't own an automobile, can't even drive one—do you think he should pay for highways for overloaded trucks that tear up the highways faster than you can build them? We got a coffee-ground formation in south Louisiana—it cost three times more to build a road in south Louisiana than it does in west Texas—but still the *Picayune* says they don't know, they can't understand. Well, there's a hell of a lot that they don't understand—that they *do* understand but they don't want *you* to understand. And you can say this, as long as I've got the breath and the life and the health, I've got the fortitude and the backbone to tell 'em, and dammit they know I'll tell 'em, and that's why they're against me. You can only judge the future by the past."

Almost all the elements of the Long appeal are there, starting with the pensions, which Huey conceived and sponsored, and on which a high proportion of the elderly people in Louisiana live—seventy-two dollars a month now, a fine sum in a low-income state. "But still the *Picayune* says they don't know, they can't understand" refers to the good roads whose high price the *Times-Picayune* constantly carps at, because, the Longs always imply, the *Picayune*, organ of the czarists, secretly wants *bad* roads. "They know I'll tell them,

and that's why they're against me" means that the press—a
monopoly press in New Orleans now—has always been against
the Longs, the champions of the poor; when all the press
consistently opposes one skillful man, he can turn its opposition into a backhanded testimony to his unique virtue.

"You can only judge the future by the past" is a reminder
that the past in Louisiana, before Huey, was painful for the
small farmers in the northern hills and along the southern
bayous. It is not hard to select such an all-inclusive passage
from a Long speech; they recur constantly, the mixture as
before.

Then followed clips showing the crucial scrimmages on
the floor of the Legislature. In the beginning, I could see,
the Governor was as confident as Oedipus Tyrannus before
he got the bad news. He felt a giant among pygmies, a pike
among crappies, as he stood there among the legislators,
most of whom owed him for favors—special bills passed for
their law clients, state jobs for constituents, "contributions"
for their personal campaign funds, and so on. But that day the
Governor was rushing in where the dinner-party liberals who
represent one or two Southern states in Washington have
steadily refused to tread. Old Earl was out to liberalize the
registration law, passed in Reconstruction times, that gives
parish (i.e., county) registrars the power to disqualify voters
arbitrarily on "educational" grounds. Except in a few rural
parishes, the effect of this law has been on the decline for
decades, but now a white-supremacy group in the legislature
had moved for its strict enforcement—against colored voters,
of course. It took me a minute or two to realize that the old
"demagogue" was actually making a civil-rights speech.

"Now, this registration you're talking about," he said. "That was put through in carpetbag days, when colored people and scalawags were running rampant in our country. You got to interpret the Constitution. There ain't ten people looking at me, including myself, who, if properly approached or attacked, could properly qualify to vote. They say this a nigger bill—ain't no such." (The old law, if enforced impartially, would also have disqualified a number—large but hard to estimate—of older white men and women who had been on the rolls since they were twenty-one but were not Ph.Ds. Needless to say, the bill's proponents did not expect enforcement to be impartial.)

At this point, the camera focused on a young man with slick black hair and a long upper lip who was wearing a broad necktie emblazoned with a Confederate flag and who addressed a microphone with gestures appropriate to mass meetings. "It's Willie Rainach, the Citizens' Council boy," one of my mentors told me. Rainach, who is a state senator from Summerfield, in Claiborne Parish, pleaded with his colleagues not to let Long "sell Louisiana down the river." (I felt another concept crumbling; I had always thought it was Negroes who got sold down rivers.)

Long, grabbing for a microphone—probably he had no legal right to be in the argument at all—remonstrated, "I think there's such a thing as being overeducated. Scientists tell me there's enough wrinkles up there—" tapping his head—"to take care of all kinds of stuff. Maybe I'm getting old—I'm losing some of mine. I hope that don't happen to Rainach. After all this over, he'll probably go up there to Summerfield, get up on his front porch, take off his shoes, wash his feet, look at the moon and get close to God." This was gross comedy, a piece of miming that recalled Jimmy Savo impersonating the Mississippi River. Then the old man, changing pace, shouted in Rainach's direction, "And when you *do,* you got to *re*cognize that *niggers* is human beings!"

It was at this point that the legislators must have decided he'd gone off his crumpet. Old Earl, a Southern politician, was taking the Fourteenth Amendment's position that "No State shall make or enforce any law which shall abridge the privileges or immunities of citizens of the United States . . . nor deny to any person within its jurisdiction the equal protection of the laws." So sporadic was my interest in Southern matters then that I did not know the Federal Department of Justice had already taken action against Washington Parish, over near the Mississippi line, because the exponents of the law that Earl didn't like had scratched the names of 1,377 Negro voters, out of a total of 1,510, from the rolls. (When, in January 1960, six months later, United States District Judge J. Skelly Wright, a Louisianian, ordered the Negroes' names put back on the rolls, no dispatch clapped old Earl on the back for having championed them. Nor, in February, when Louisiana appealed Judge Wright's decision and the Supreme Court sustained it, did anybody give the old battler credit for having battled. The main feature of the civil-rights bill passed by Congress was, in fact, an affirmation of the Earl Long argument that led to his sojourn in Texas, but nobody recalled the trouble that his fight for civil rights had cost him.)

"There's no longer *slavery!*" Long shouted at Rainach. "There wasn't but two people in Winn Parish that was able

to own slaves—one was my grandpa, the other was my uncle—
and when they were freed, they stayed on" (here his voice
went tenor and sentimental, then dropped again) "and two
of those fine old colored women more or less died in my
Christian mother's arms—Black Alice and Aunt Rose." He
sounded like a blend of David Warfield and Morton Downey.
"To keep fine, honorable grayheaded men and women off
the registration rolls, some of whom have been voting as
much as sixty or sixty-five years—I plead with you in all
candor. I'm a candidate for Governor. If it hurts me, it will
just have to hurt."

He didn't believe it would hurt, but it did. In any case, he
was taking a chance, which put him in a class by himself
among Southern public men.

This was the high point of the Governor's performance,
an Elizabethan juxtaposition of comedy and pathos; weeks
after witnessing it, I could still visualize Senator Rainach up
on his porch in Summerfield, looking at the moon, foot in
hand, and feeling integrated with his Creator. As the session
continued, the old man, blundering into opposition he hadn't
expected, became bitter and hardly coherent.

The theme of one long passage was that many legislators
had Negro or at least part-Negro relatives in the bar sinister
category, to whom they now wanted to deny the vote. He told
a story about his own uncle who, climbing into bed with a
Negro woman, had given umbrage to her husband, then
present.

Here the Governor's voice was sad, like the voice of a man
recounting the death of Agamemnon: "He shot my poor
uncle—" a one-beat pause—"and he died." If white men had

let Negro women alone, he said, there wouldn't be any trouble.

The squabble continued, Uncle Earl growing progressively less effective, but with flashes of humor: of some fellow on his own side, he said once, "Why does the *Picayune* hate him —is why I like him. When he makes the *Picayune* scratch and wiggle, he is putting anointed oil on my head."

The others snarled him down, and Mrs. Dixon led him from the floor.

The light in the projection room went on, as if at the end of a first act, and there was a pause while the operator loaded a new reel. When the show went on again, I saw a shocking change. The Governor, between his exit from the screen and his reappearance, had made the tortuous journey to Texas and back. Extended on a pallet in a dusty little hotel at Covington, where he lay after winning his way to freedom by firing the hospital officials, he recalled old newsreel shots of Mahatma Gandhi. His pale, emaciated arms and chest showed over the top of a sheet that covered the rest of his body, and he addressed the reporters in a hoarse whisper that was hard to understand because he had mislaid his dentures. It was the beginning of the second chapter of the legend of Long-family martyrdom: following the assassination of Huey, the crucifixion of Earl.

"I'm very happy to be relieved from hijacking, kidnaping, punctures, needles, and everything they could use," he said, "and one of the first things I'm going to do is see that no person, colored or white or what, has to go through the same humiliation, the same intimidation, the same hurts and

bruises that I did. I think it was politics—I think some of my
enemies thought that this was a way to get rid of old Uncle
Earl.

"In my opinion, instead of hurting me politically, I think
this is going to make me," the old boy moaned happily, trans-
muting his hurts into votes even as he ached, "I b'lieve our
state and nation needs a few senior statesmen to hold the
younger ones down—when you get to be sixty you realize
what it's all about."

Here he closed his eyes, as if in mystic prayer, and one of
the Faithful around him, a woman with a big chin, hauled
off and recited W. E. Henley's "Invictus," the Long family
anthem since Huey's day—it was the only poem Huey ever
liked.

His appearance and weakness at this interview had set
many reporters to predicting that his death was imminent.
But his performances within the next month had stimulated
a counter-rumor that the whole episode was from beginning
to end a fake, put on to build up a defense against income-tax
prosecution. The second report credited its hero with a yogi's
gift of physical retraction—he had lost another thirty pounds
between the Baton Rouge and Covington scenes.

Now, in a motel near Covington, a day later, he was on the
subject of his wife, talking with a touch more vigor as he
picked up strength: "There hasn't been a woman employed
by me that she didn't worry about—any decent, nice-looking
woman. How can an old man like me take care of three or
four of them when I'd do well to take care of one and know
I'm doing a bum job at that—that's why she tried to get rid
of me—I don't blame her."

The next sequence was pastoral—on the veranda of Earl's old-fashioned farm at Winnfield, in his home parish, where it is politically inadvisable to paint the house too often. The horrors of Texas and Mandeville were beginning to recede. "Now I'm at my little ol' peapatch farm in Winnfield, where I raise some billy goats, shoats, cows, got two or three old plug horses, but they suit me," he said. "I knew I was a little run down in the Legislature. Only two weeks to go, and I knew there was lots of important things that would fall if I wasn't there. When they kidnaped me, I lost the loan-shark bill." This was a bill to regulate rates of interest charged by small-loan companies, and the Governor's tone made me tremble for the small debtors of Louisiana, left naked to the exactions of the Shylocks.

The respite at Winnfield was brief, however—just a couple of days, while he prepared for a few nonpolitical, pre-campaign stump speeches. The screen showed one of these stump appearances, too. The Governor was weak and had to be helped up some wooden steps set against the side of the flat-bodied truck from which he spoke. The sun, to judge from the sweaty faces of the crowd, must have been killing. He didn't say much; the main purpose of his appearances was to show the voters that Lazarus was in business at the old stand. Joe Arthur Sims, his disciple-at-law, made the principal speech. Mr. Sims is a big young man, about six feet four, with a big face windowed in tortoise shell, a big chin, and a big voice.

His delivery is based on increasing volume, like the noise of an approaching subway train; when he reaches his climaxes, you feel almost irresistibly impelled to throw yourself flat between the rails and let the cars pass over you. "When our beloved friend, the *fine* Governor of the Gret Stet of Loosiana, sent for me in his need at Mandeville," Mr. Sims said, "his condition had been *so* MISREPRESENTED—" here he took the train around a loop and up to Seventy-second Street before he started down again—"that people I knew said to me, 'Don't you go up there, Joe Sims. That man is a *hyena*. He'll BITE YOU IN THE LAIG.' But I went. I went to Mandeville, and before I could reach my friend, *the armed guard had to open ten locked doors,* and lock each one of 'em again after us. And theah, *theah,* I found the FINE Governor, of the GRET Stet of Loosiana—" and here his shocked voice backed up way beyond Columbus Circle—"without SHOES, without a stitch of CLOTHES to put awn him, without a friend to counsel with. And he was just as rational as he has ever been in his life, or as you see him here today. He said, 'JOE SIMS, WHERE THE HELL YOU BEEN?'"

CHAPTER II

HE'S AN IMAM

When Tom and the lawyer and I left the projection room, I felt that I had been introduced into a new world, and it gave me something to think about as we moved from cool WDSU through the wet heat toward Pete Herman's bar. The transitions between conditioned and unconditioned air are the new pattern of life in the summer South. This was a pilgrimage. Herman (his name in the prize ring), who has been blind for thirty-seven years, was the best infighter I have ever seen in my life, and I had to tell him so. As I age, I grow more punctilious about my aesthetic debts; in Paris a few years ago I met Arthur Waley and thanked him for translating the *Tale of Genji*. I had watched Herman fight fifteen rounds against Midget Smith at the old Madison Square Garden during my college holidays in December of 1921. They were bantamweights—a hundred and eighteen pounds. Herman was already nearly blind, although he was not saying so. He fought by a system of feint and touch. Until he could make

contact, he would move his head to draw Smith's punches
to where he did not mean to be, and then, as soon as he felt
a glove or an arm or a passing current of air, he knew where
he was. If he had his glove on a man's right biceps, he knew
where the man's left hand and belly and chin must be as a
touch typist knows where the letters are on the keyboard. He
could anticipate moves, and lead and counter and put his
combinations of blows together at a range of inches; I have
heard it said that he could feint, and fool you, with both
hands out of sight. At the Garden, I could see the beauty of
what he was doing, but I couldn't understand why, when he
hurt Smith, he didn't follow him up. And until he had established touch again, Herman was lost; Smith, a tough little
slugger, caught him with some savage blows that Herman—
inexplicably, then—failed to see, although they were a long
way coming. Smith got the decision, but I thought it unjust,
and until Herman's manager announced Pete's retirement
because of blindness, I lacked the key to what I had witnessed.
In the thirty-nine years since, I have never seen such a performance. "What Pete Herman done," an initiate once told
me, with awe, "nobody could have learned him." My New
Orleans companions, both of whom were children when
Herman was fighting, could not fathom my compulsion to
see him; they probably thought he was like what you see on
television. To them he was only a hard little Italian named
Gulotta, whose late brother, Gaspar, had been the official
collector of the contributions to police and politicians that
kept the sucker traps in the Quarter operating.

Pete's joint was a bar that had a back room with a floor
show. The show was on when we arrived. There were only

a couple of people in the bar, but the back room was packed. A Negro, who the master of ceremonies said was named Pork Chops, was dancing desultorily, and he and the M.C. were carrying on a dialogue:

M.C.: If you're so good, why aren't you on television?

P.C.: I'm waiting for *colored* television.

With this, everybody except us got up and left, in a disciplined, joyless group. I hadn't thought the joke was that bad, and I was almost glad the proprietor was blind, because otherwise the exodus might have hurt his feelings. But then I learned that such mass entrances and departures are routine, like the alternations of being too hot or too cold. The migrating audiences are tourists from Iowa, who sign up for rounds of the night clubs at their hotels and are carried from one joint to the next in buses. The deal apparently includes one soft drink at each stop.

When the sightseers had gone, we sent for the proprietor, who came over to us, walking briskly and only once or twice checking his course by touching a table. He had a big head and a welterweight's shoulders and thorax on short legs—a jockey's build. I told him I had seen him fight Midget Smith. "And I still think you should have had the decision," I said.

"I thought I win, too," he agreed. "I could see Smith was cut up bad." I assumed that his manager had told him Smith was cut up bad. Then he said happily, "Barney Ross was in here a couple of weeks ago with a fighter he's handling. Barney's thirteen years younger than me, and he looks older. He's gone all gray on top." Then I understood that he visualizes what people tell him and that a minute later it's all a part of his past, as if he'd seen it himself. Pretty soon he excused himself and went about his business, as a good saloon-keeper should. When he was gone, we had a round of beer and began talking about the Governor again.

"Don't let him con you," the lawyer said. "You hoid him talk about, yeah, Black Alice, and, yeah, Aunt Rose, but all he cares about is Uncle Oil." There is a New Orleans city accent (which I shall try to reproduce only fitfully) associated with downtown New Orleans, particularly with the German and Irish Third Ward, that is hard to distinguish from the accent of Hoboken, Jersey City, and Astoria, Long Island, where the Al Smith inflection, extinct in Manhattan, has taken refuge. The reason, as you might expect, is that the same stocks that brought the accent to Manhattan imposed it on New Orleans, between the eighteen-forties and the Civil War. Irish immigrants, not Negro slaves, built the levees; the Negroes, bought at high prices to work cotton, were too valuable to use on low-pay labor. "Earl doesn't care about the jigs," the lawyer went on. "He wants their votes. And he knows he'll get them if he can just make those other fellows keep their hands off the lists. They're just fakers anyway. They don't want to disfranchise all niggers—only his niggers. When they've got a nigger they can be sure of, they'll vote him every time. Uncle Earl makes sweet talk about keeping those old white people on the lists, too. He knows that any man or woman old enough to draw a pension will vote for a Long every time. And that loan-shark bill he talks about—hell, he just doesn't want to let that small-loan business out from under his thumb. It's too rich. The small-loan companies are licensed to lend sums up to a thousand now. The bill would have limited the interest on loans of under a thousand to three and a half per cent a month—that's forty-two per cent a year. But it would have given them the right to make loans of more than a thousand dollars at true loan-shark rates. The loan business of over a thousand is reserved for the banks now. So Earl's loan-shark bill would have helped the sharks more than it hurt them. I'll bet the sharks were *for* it, and the *banks* put up the money to fight it."

I said I couldn't understand the importance of the small-loan firms to a politician. We have them in New York, but they are not considered important sources of graft.

"It's because to get a license for a small-loan company you have to get a special bill passed through the Legislature and signed by the Governor," the lawyer explained impatiently. "One Shylock, one bill. It's the surest way in the world to get rich. So a man wants a small-loan license, he goes to a politician from his home parish and gives him ten thousand dollars to take up to Baton Rouge. The fellow steers it through—he gives so much here and so much there, and maybe a good campaign contribution to whoever's Governor for signing. And what's left sticks to him for his trouble. There've been seventy-two special small-loan bills passed and signed in the last couple of sessions. So now comes a bill to change the statute itself—you can *imagine* the number of jackpots there are to be split up. What makes Uncle Earl sore is that they run him off to Texas before he could get into the act. He wants his leaders to be like those trained dogs you used to see in vaudeville—the ones that hold a pose until the trainer tells them to come and get their piece of meat."

"Earl likes to cut them down to size before they get too big and fresh," Tom Sancton said. "You heard what he did to

the fellow from Alexandria who got a big retainer from the
theater owners to try to remove a two per cent tax on movie
admissions? The fellow went to see Earl before the last
campaign and came back and told his clients that it was in
the bag. Then he went out and worked like a dog for Earl—
speaking on television and radio, and stumping and con-
spiring and kissing babies and hustling votes—until Earl was
elected Governor. One of the first things Earl did in the new
Legislature was to *oppose* removal of the tax. The fellow
from Alexandria went to see him—he was afraid he would
have to refund his fee, or the theater owners would shoot
him—and he said, 'I told my clients that you said you wanted
their support and that you wouldn't block removal of the tax.
What do I tell them now?' You know what old Earl said? He
said, 'I'll tell you what to tell them. Tell them I lied.' "

"Why did he do that?" I asked. "Did somebody induce
him to *keep* the tax on the movies?"

"Hell, no," said Tom. "He just didn't want the other
fellow's clients to think the other fellow was that strong. He
likes them to come straight to Uncle Earl." Tom, who is
impressed by medical opinion, added: "I'm afraid he won't
make it this time, though. My doctor told me that what the
man needs is about six months of solid rest in a sanitarium
if he wants to live."

"Rest is just what might kill him," I said. I have always believed in the therapeutic value of attending horse races. It
fills the lungs and empties the mind. You sit a horseplayer
down to occupational therapy and he will founder.

"Oh, there's lots of ways of making money here," the lawyer said, returning to what interested him. He left pathology

to them that liked it. "For instance, a law says that all state property must be insured at a rate set by a committee known as the Louisiana Insurance Rating and Fire Agency. That does away with competitive bidding, so placing insurance is just a matter of dealer's choice. The Federal Housing Authority has found that on public housing, built partly with Federal and partly with state funds, the insurance rate here is the highest in the nation. And then there's the tax payable to the state on sulphur taken from the ground. It's set ridiculously low—one dollar and three cents a ton—by a provision of the state constitution. There isn't a session of the Legislature that somebody doesn't introduce a sulphur bill to amend the constitution. It's always beaten—but just. How much does it cost the sulphur companies to keep that limit on the books?"

"But old Earl is tight with his money," Sancton said. "The one thing he's never been tight about is horse betting. He can't stop. When he gets the papers in the morning, he tears them open and goes straight to the hog quotations and the racing charts. After that, he gets a batch of *Daily Racing Forms* and *Morning Telegraphs* and lays out the entries and past performances at every track going—side by side, on a long table. It's too much trouble to use one paper and turn the pages. Then he goes to work with a red pencil and a blue one, and in an hour or so he begins calling up touts on long distance—Picklenosed Willie and The Owl and Stableboy and fellows like that. Next, he starts calling bookies to place his bets—a few dollars on each of three horses in practically every race in the country, unless one of the touts has given him something hot, and then he lays it in. If he's betting a book in Louisiana and he loses, he puts it on the tab, but if he wins, he has a state trooper over at the bookie's joint within a half hour to collect."

This was the life I had always wanted to live, and I had a great fellow feeling for Uncle Earl as the lawyer took up the refrain.

"After he makes his bets, the day's business can begin," the lawyer said. "First item is to turn to the supermarket ads. If he sees something in the ads that the price is right, he buys it regardless if he needs it at the moment or not. Like the morning he saw that Schwegmann's was selling potatoes for forty-nine cents a ten-pound sack. Schwegmann's is a string of three big supermarkets here that sell everything—furniture, automobile parts, grits, steak. Earl was a couple of days out of the State Hospital and was staying here at the Roosevelt Hotel with ten state policemen, and there were a dozen politicians paying their respects. Earl says, 'Come on, boys, I can't afford to pass that up,' and he goes downstairs and gets into his eleven-thousand-dollar air-conditioned official Cadillac that he says he got for eighty-five hundred because he is always protecting the interest of the fine people of the Great State of Louisiana, and the state troopers get out in front on motorcycles to clear the way, and he sits in front, next to the chauffeur, the way he always does, and packs those politicians in the back, and they take off. They pull up in front of Schwegmann's—all the sirens blowing, frightening hell out of the other shoppers—and Earl gets out and heads straight for the vegetable department, and, yeah, there are the potato sacks, but they're marked fifty cents instead of forty-nine. Earl calls for the store manager and accuses him of mislead-

ing advertising and shows him the ad, and the manager calls
over all the clerks he can spare, and they change the price on
the bags from fifty cents to forty-nine. That satisfies Earl, so
he buys a hundred pounds of the potatoes and tells a state
senator to pick them up and carry them to the car, and then
he sees some alarm clocks on sale and buys three hundred
dollars' worth, and tells some representatives from upcountry
to carry them. And eighty-seven dozen goldfish in individual
plastic bags of water, and two cases of that sweet Mogen David
wine, and he tells the new superintendent of state police to
load up. By the time they come out it looks like a safari, with
all them politicians as native bearers. He must have had five
thousand dollars' worth of junk."

"What did he think he was going to do with the stuff?" I
asked.

"Damfino," the lawyer said. "It's just one of his ideas of
pleasure. Well, when they got out there on the sidewalk,
under about a hundred degrees of heat, the stuff won't all go
in the trunk of the Cadillac. At least, the trunk won't close.
So Uncle Earl sends a couple of senators and a judge into
the store again to buy some rope, and they can't find any but
the gold kind that women use to tie back drapes with, so they
buy about a furlong of that, and then when they get outside,
the Cadillac is so low-slung they can't pass the rope under the
car. By that time Uncle Earl is sitting in his air-cooled seat
eating watermelon with salt, and he orders the chauffeur to
get out and tell the judge to lie down under the car and get
the rope around the best he can. The judge gets down on
his knees, and as he does he says, 'I wonder what the gover-

nors of the forty-nine other states are doing right this minute!' "

Louisianians often tell this story, and they never fail to
laugh at it. It could be the subject of a Daumier lithograph,
and they have a Daumier sense of humor.

"And who are the candidates who are going to run against
Uncle Earl?" I asked, almost as an afterthought. All the conversation I had heard that evening sounded as if Uncle Earl
were running against hardened arteries, cerebral accidents,
his wife, exhaustion, and the investigative branch of the
Internal Revenue Service.

"Well," Sancton said, "there's Chep Morrison, the Mayor
of New Orleans—he's the one Uncle Earl calls Dellasoups.
He's a brisk, nice-looking fellow, and his boosters say he gets
things done, but he has two strikes against him out of town—
he's a Catholic and he's a New Orleans man. As Mayor of
New Orleans he's made himself an international figure, tour-
ing South America and Europe to get business for the port,
and he's improved the city physically, but the kind of mayor
who looks right taking Zsa Zsa Gabor to tea looks all wrong
to those rednecks up in the hill parishes. Being a Catholic
doesn't hurt him downstate—our Cajuns are Catholics, too,
of course—but being from New Orleans does hurt. And even
in the city he beat Uncle Earl by only twenty-two hundred
votes in 1956. Of course, if Earl was out, Chep would carry
the city big, and he'd get all the Negro vote; Earl gets about
two thirds of it now and Chep the rest. And he'd get the
organized-labor vote, too—but only if Earl was out. He would
have been Mayor for life, but in 1952 the city passed a law
that no mayor of New Orleans could succeed himself more

than once. Chep backed the new law, and maybe he wishes
now he hadn't, like the Republicans who pushed the no-
third-term amendment for President.

"Then there's Bill Dodd, the state comptroller. Big Bad
Bill Dodd, Uncle Earl calls him. Dodd is an old Long man.
He was Lieutenant Governor with Earl from 1948 to 1952,
and ran for comptroller on the same ticket with him in 1956,
but they're enemies now. With Earl out, he'd get most of the
steady Long vote. And there's Willie Rainach, the racist, but
he won't get anybody but his own kind. The race issue isn't
as hot in Louisiana as it is in Arkansas or Alabama or Mississippi. Nobody will say he's *for* integration in the schools, but
as for letting Negroes vote or not vote, most people are for
leaving things as they are—a kind of local option. Morrison
and old Uncle Earl might lose some votes by being what people call a little 'soft on the niggers,' but those people wouldn't
necessarily all go to Rainach—many would go to somebody
in between."

"That's why a lot of people think Jimmie Davis is the best
bet," the lawyer broke in. "Jimmie is a psalm-singing fellow
from up in Shreveport, in the northwest corner of the state.
He used to be a hillbilly singer and composer—he wrote
'You Are My Sunshine, My Only Sunshine'—and he was Governor from 1944 to 1948. He isn't a clown; he's smart. Lately
he's been making a lot of religious records. That helps him
with the church people, and when he was Governor he didn't
have any trouble with the gamblers either. His motto is 'I
Never Done Nobody No Harm.' Davis is a country boy from
a big city, but Shreveport doesn't frighten the rubes the way
New Orleans does. If he could get into the second primary

with either Earl or Chep, he might inherit the votes of all the candidates who lost out."

The one political element that neither of my mentors mentioned even once—nor did they need to—was the Republican party. It is the smallest of all the political sects in Louisiana. In the statewide primaries of 1956, there were seven hundred and forty thousand Democratic voters and eighteen hundred and eighty-three Republican voters. There are no Republican watchers at most polling places on primary day, because there aren't enough Republicans to go around. Of the eighteen hundred and eighty-three Republican voters, it is my impression that eighteen hundred and eighty-two are lawyers, and during a Republican administration in Washington, at least three quarters of them have Federal jobs. Aspirants to the order have to be of sober demeanor and sterling character, to live down the ripe odor left by the "Customhouse" Republican regime of Reconstruction days, so called because President Grant's brother-in-law, James F. Casey, was Collector of Customs for New Orleans.

Known as the party of plunder when they were turned out in 1876, the Republicans have become the party of purity in state affairs. Louisiana Republicans must also have better than average education, because of the high incidence of office they must cope with when the wind off the Potomac is favorable. Barring protracted accidents like Roosevelt-Truman, a Louisiana Republican has three hundred and ninety-eight times the chances of a Louisiana Democrat to become a Federal judge. Patience and self-denial are other necessary qualifications, since the novice renounces all hope of elective office when he takes the veil. His salvation can only come from

outside the state, as Zeus came to Danae in a shower of gold.
But it comes quite often. Since 1876, when Washington
abandoned the Reconstruction, Republicans have held the
White House and its appointive powers for forty-eight out of
eighty-four years.

I never learned the process of induction into the Louisiana Republican cult, but the ranks are always full, and the
queue does not disperse when there are long waits between
buses. Even during these spells of unemployment, the Republicans suffer no outrage. No Democrat in his right mind wants
to incur the wrath of a man who will be a United States
District Judge or a District Director of Internal Revenue
the next time the Republicans win. Like the Parsees in India
and the Mozabites in Algeria, they have won respect as clean,
sober and industrious people, and their attorneys get a full
share of civil practice.

"And who is your man?" I asked my two mentors.

The lawyer, who had been knocking the Governor ever
since I met him, said, as if there had never been any doubt of
where he stood, "I'll stay with Uncle Earl unless he looks too
sick to go the distance. They may say, yeah, he's crazy, and,
yeah, he's got deep pockets, and, yeah, he'd cut his best
friend's throat to keep him from getting elected, but how
far do you think a man like me would have got in the Louisiana bar before Huey came along? Up from the bottom, ate
my way free through college by playing football, studied
law at night. Without the Longs I'd be limited to police-
court cases. Any time I walked into court against one of those
old-family boys from the big law firms that represented the
banks and oil companies, I'd be dead."

The lawyer is a member of the Regular Democratic Organization, the New Orleans machine that is the spiritual equivalent of old-fashioned Tammany Hall. The Old Regulars, as they are known, fought Huey Long until he broke their power in the thirties and then joined him. "Before Huey," the lawyer went on, "the state was as tight as a drum and crooked as a corkscrew; now it's still crooked, but it's open to everybody. Maybe some judges do cut up jackpots, but they aren't working for a monopoly. In business it's the same—there's plenty of ex-wildcatters, oil-and-gas millionaires, who under the old house rules would have been crushed out before they got started. Huey was like the kid who comes along in a game of Chicago pool when all the balls are massed. He breaks them and runs a few, then misses and leaves the table full of shots for the other players. As long as the Longs are in, you have a chance."

"You got to remember that Earl carries the blood of Huey the Martyr," Sancton said. "He's an Imam. People up North see Huey's career from the wrong end. Here, a lot of voters remember him as a poor, friendless boy who stood up to the bully—the rich machine that had run Louisiana forever. He licked it. That put him in a favorable light. By the time the North's attention was attracted to Huey, he was sitting on the bully's chest. That made *him* look like the bully. The papers called for law and order, and when that fellow shot Huey in the Capitol, they said law and order had been vindicated."

CHAPTER III

BRUTTALLY FRANK

Maneuvers like Earl's scheme to succeed himself un-immediately enrage the Longs' opponents because they never think of them first. The opposition is personified by the rich and conservative *Times-Picayune* and its afternoon satellite, the *States-Item* (these hyphenated newspaper titles, memorials to cannibalism, are becoming a rule rather than the exception in a shrinking press). The double-barreled duo is continually getting mad at the Longs, like a fat policeman in an old-time silent film shaking his fist at Charlie Chaplin. Chaplin in the films always ran around the block and kicked the policeman in the pants, and, like the little man in the bowler, the Longs always enlist popular sympathy. This would be harder to understand in a state other than Louisiana, where the populace has always viewed its self-acknowledged betters with skeptical animosity.

The anti-Longites' fair-haired boy for thirteen years, up to and including the summer of 1959, was Mayor Morrison.

I thought that I ought to talk to him to see what the Martyr was up against. I had heard that Morrison bragged of a private poll that showed him a winner with 52.78 per cent of all votes cast in the first primary for Governor, whether Long ran or not. This would insure his election as Governor without need of a runoff primary. The consensus in New Orleans' political cafés, however—a term signifying any place in town where you can buy a cup of coffee—was that he was desperate and talking through his tuppy.

"He has to go up or out," one expert said. "The fat cats who paid for his campaign for Governor in 1956 are discouraged. His charm doesn't work upstate."

The Mayor, known to the general public as Chep, is a city type. I had heard admirers, chiefly public-relations men for the city, describe him as a melange of Jimmy Walker for looks and manner, Fiorello La Guardia for energy and probity, and Big Bad Bob Moses, the Builder, for getting things done.

People who didn't like him conceded only the energy and a certain hard neatness of appearance. They said he was terrifyingly ambitious, a complete egoist and willing to trade for votes anywhere. The gamblers and brothel keepers accused him of a double cross; before his first election, in 1946, they said, he had caused them to understand that his reformism was a sham and that if he was elected they could continue to operate wide open, *without* paying graft to the Old Regular machine.

After election he had shut them down, to consolidate his position with the church- and womenfolk. That had continued until he copyrighted the label of respectability in New

Orleans, so that to run against him was like running for
office against a coalition of the Holy Ghost *and* the *Times-
Picayune*. Meanwhile he used municipal patronage to build
up a machine that could compete with the Old Regulars.

A good number of the saloonkeepers, figuring they wouldn't
lick him, joined him in return for a kind of modified autonomy—about what De Gaulle has been offering to the
Algerians. New Orleans, while no Gomorrah, is certainly not
a sedate town now. Cab drivers wait at the exits of the strip-
tease joints to proposition the visiting firemen, rendered
randy by the bumps and grinds. The cabbies pimp for the
brothels across the river in Jefferson Parish. The cops operate
like the New York Police during Prohibition—they move
aggrieved drunks along rather than listen to their beefs.

At a dinner of Morrison people to which I was invited, a
charming downstate lady, counted upon as a sure source of
Morrison campaign money, alarmed her hosts by saying that
she was about through wasting cash on Blue Boy, a nick-
name for Morrison that in itself showed a deterioration of
his sentimental appeal. When, at thirty-four, he first won the
mayoralty, an inspired female admirer called him Little
Boy Blue, blowing his own horn to rally the forces of decency. Now, at forty-seven, he was just Blue Boy, a name evok-
ing blue babies and blue chins.

The lady and her husband are both as physically abundant
as they are agreeable—two rich people who look like rich
people, with not a concavity in their contours and not a
regret in their heads about being so rich.

"I don't mind the money," she said, "but I just hate having
a loser. My husband can go on backing Blue Boy if he wants,

but I'm going with Jimmie Davis." Her husband smiled deprecatingly, but he did not look like a man fond of backing losers indefinitely, either. The lady's announcement spread dismay among the Morrison professionals. (Later, she came back to Morrison, but the ripples stirred by her threat could not be recalled.)

I was to see the Mayor next morning at City Hall, and I arrived early for my appointment. The City Hall itself is a monument to the Morrison administration, as the Capitol at Baton Rouge is a monument to Huey Long's. An assistant to the Mayor, a Mr. Dixon, showed me over the place before His Honor showed up. We ended our tour in the Council Chamber, a modest vault of marble and blond tropical woods —woods from all the countries with which New Orleans traded, Mr. Dixon said. The difference between the porphyry and agate of the State House and the blond mahogany of City Hall is the difference between the Long-family and Morrison manner. Morrison has better taste—but not by Louisiana standards.

"Each session of the Council is opened with prayer by a minister of one of the three great faiths, Catholic, Protestant and Hebrew," Mr. Dixon said reverentially. "They take it in rotation." With an arrangement like that, the great city of New Orleans, like a prudent oil man, had money on each of the three leading candidates. I tapped my breast, to make sure my wallet was still with me.

When we emerged from this air-cooled crypt, refreshed and feeling slightly sanctified, we returned to the mayoral suite, where representatives of the entire local press awaited us— a man from the *Times-Picayune* and a girl from the *States-*

Item, like a racing entry marked 1 and 1A. With three or
four secretaries, a photographer and Tom, we filed into the
Mayor's audience room.

It was paneled with double- or treble-autographed photographs of the Mayor with the last Pope, Perón, Trujillo,
Cardinal Spellman, Bishop Fulton J. Sheen, a number of
prominent race horses and various Gabor sisters. There were
also United States Senators, baseball players, television personalities, and a number of Miss New Orleanses, Miss Loui-
sianas and Miss Confederate Daughters of America. There
was a picture of Mayor Morrison in a colonel's uniform at
the Eiffel Tower after he liberated it in 1944, and snaps of
him laying cornerstones and greeting a delegation of Uru-
guayan school children. In all of them he was smiling and
fighting politely for the center of the picture, even at the
risk of being trampled by a horse. I found the entire display
an engaging disclaimer of false modesty.

When I had browsed awhile, we all sat down, and a colored
man brought us coffee. The ceremonial coffee is a link between Louisiana and the rest of the Arab world. It is never
omitted, even though your host is going to throw you out
when you have drunk it.

We had no sooner put our cups down than the Mayor entered briskly, smiling, wearing a dazzling suit of tropical
cloth and a necktie like a Persian dawn. He is a man in
appearance midway between Richard M. Nixon and John
F. Kennedy, and as tenacious of youth.

At an age when prize fighters are described as venerable
freaks, politicians are still referred to as "young." In an
effort to live up to the adjective, most politicos in their forties

act downright kittenish. This puts an increasing burden on them with the years, for no performer wants his public to notice that he is aging. It is an advantage to a man who aims high not to project a public image until he is bald or gray, has a few wrinkles on his face, and is too slow to show that he is slowing up. So the great Bob Fitzsimmons, bald from youth, did not buy a toupee to make him look younger, but raised a long mustache to make him look older. Ten years later he shaved it off, and contemporaries said he looked as young as when he first came over from Australia. Grand Old Juvenile is a hard role to sustain, even with the aid of geriatrics. If I were coaching a candidate in the Nixon-Morrison-Kennedy age range, I would bid him raise mutton-chop whiskers and cultivate a limp, so that when the inevitable happened the deterioration would be less striking.

This, however, is a digression. In New Orleans, Mr. Dixon hauled at my sleeve and, when I rose, moved me into a corner of the office where I had my back to a big American flag and my left side toward the Mayor, who with practiced adroitness placed one side of a document the size of a large bill of fare in my right hand. I tried to read it, but the printed side was toward the camera.

The Mayor smiled. The photographer blazed away. The whole operation could not have taken more than thirty-two seconds, and I was now, as I ascertained when I had a chance to read the bill of fare, an "Honorary Citizen of New Orleans, the International City founded in 1718 A.D. by the French Explorer Bienville . . . a city of Old World Tradition and New World Enterprise famed for its charm, beauty and hospitality . . . one of America's most progressive communities . . . a great World Port and the center of a vast and growing industrial empire. . . ." I also got a gold-plated "key to the city."

What impressed me about the operation was its practiced efficiency. They had my name spelled right, as if they had been waiting for me to come along. All around the text were lithographed vignettes of New Orleans glories, most of them reflecting credit on Morrison; the new City Hall and civic center, built under Morrison; the Moisant International Airport Terminal, erected *au temps de Morrison*; the new Mississippi Bridge, built during a Morrison term of office; the International Home and Trade Mart, completed while Morrison was Mayor; and the new Union Passenger Terminal, uniting the Illinois Central and Louisville and Nashville stations under one roof in the center of the city, a monument to the Morrison regime. Other vignettes were devoted to the port, which the Mayor has done much to develop, and the skyline, in which he takes a proprietary interest.

"World famous Cuisine and Birthplace of Jazz," and "Vieux Carré and Mardi Gras," and the football stadium were the only depicted attractions that were not directly attributable to the Mayor—three out of ten.

While I was still looking at my new diploma, Mr. Dixon, like a Billy Graham usher with a sinner in tow, led me back to my seat, at a respectful distance from the desk behind which Mayor Morrison now took station. The *Times-Picayune* man and the *States-Item* girl poised their notebooks on their respective right knees. I now realized that I had been invited not to an interview but to an audience such as Father Divine used to grant visiting sightseers in his Harlem Heaven.

The Mayor began by expressing sorrow over the plight of Governor Long. "It is to my selfish interest to have him as an opponent," he said, "because surveys show I would be a cinch to defeat him."

But, Morrison said, Old Earl was a sick man, and Louisiana couldn't afford a Governor who "wasn't even housebroke." Therefore he hoped Earl wouldn't run. The state must rebuild its prestige in the outside world if it was to attract sorely needed new industries. And he told me quite a bit about the new industries he constantly brought to New Orleans and the civic improvements he incessantly perpetrated. It was all as spontaneous as the neat diploma and the key to the city.

I stress my unfavorable first impression of Morrison because I was to wind up the campaign rooting for him with all my heart.

Tom suggested that, for balance, we call next on Jim Comiskey, the leader of the Third Ward and chief of the city-wide Old Regular Democratic organization. Morrison kept the municipal patronage out of the Old Regulars' hands, Tom said, but they did well on the state patronage Earl fed them.

"The Old Regulars can't go with Morrison. They got to go with somebody from upstate. Before Earl blew his top in the Legislature, they were sitting pretty. All they had to do was sit tight with Earl and go in again. Now they don't know whether they got a candidate."

The Comiskey brothers, Jim and Larry, were wholesale liquor dealers on a mighty scale, Tom said. If we ran down to the warehouse now, we probably would catch them in.

We had best get cracking, because it was already noon, and
Jim Comiskey, if he went out to lunch, might stay out for
a siesta or take a swing around the saloons where he com-
muned with the pulse of the electorate. We climbed into
Tom's battered station wagon and raced out to where the
Comiskey Brothers' sheds and loading platforms lay under a
sun like the Sahara's. The heat bounced visibly off the con-
crete like a rubber ball. It was on a wide avenue of desolation
—railway culverts, streetcar rails, and the kind of businesses
that deal by the ton, the carboy or the freight-car load.

Jim Comiskey was not there—he was in Baton Rouge for
the day, the girl at the switchboard said—but Brother Larry
was out on the loading platform, squatting on a kitchen
chair, like a great, wise, sun-freckled toad, an old straw hat
down over his eyes, his fat red arms akimbo as he watched the
outgoing loads of lovely liquor, as hot as Tabasco sauce to
the taste, that would set longshoremen swinging their fists
and old women gabbling and Vidalias leching after *entrain-
euses* who would roll them in the dark recesses of intimate
bars. "Vidalia" is the New Orleans word for a sucker from
out of town. In the beginning it meant a rich planter from
Vidalia, up the river, in town for a good time. And on every
bottle of Comiskey's Special Private Stock Whiskey was the
photographed face of Brother Jim, like Father John on the
medicine bottle.

Brother Larry was not astonished that we had come to
consult the Oracle of the Bottle. "He's win all his life," he
said. "He knows da answers." But he disclaimed authority
to speak for the house. "Wait fa Jim," he said. And, picking
a whiskey bottle from a case, he showed me his brother's

portrait. "Dat's him," he said. It was one of the few times in
my life I have heard a pure New York accent as reported by
Stephen Crane in *Maggie*. It startled me, as if I had seen a
horse-drawn fire engine. The Third Ward lawyer's had been
diluted by education, but Larry had stayed home.

Tom had picked up another bottle and was looking at that.
Then he compared the two pictures. "Hey, they're different,"
he said. "He's smiling on one and looking sore on the other."

"Maybe he's winning easy on dis one," said Brother Larry,
"and on dat one he's in a close race. It's a wonderful free
campaign poster, dat label. A fellow is drinking and he sees
dat face on da back bar, it sinks in his conscious.

"You boys catch him at da clubhouse in da ward tomorrow
night," he said. "Every Wednesday night he's dere to hear
confessions."

"Is that what we call taking the contracts?" I asked, and
Brother Larry winked.

"Here we call it hearing confession," he said. "Everybody in da ward dat has troubles, dey come to tell dem to
Jim."

"Troubles like what?" Tom asked, in quest of the pic-
turesque detail.

"Dey all got da same one," said Brother Larry. "No money.
Dey need money. Dey're broke. Dat's da disease of da ward.
He never toins one away widout a hearing. Sometimes I've
known him to come home at five o'clock in da morning,
staying up to listen to dem."

"And what does he do for them?" I asked, although I was
sure I knew the answer. For this is an American Universal.

"He gets dem a little job," said Brother Larry. "Maybe

watchman, or laborer on a state contract, or doorman at a hospital. It don't pay much, but a man don't need much if you don't woik him too hard. It's like a mule, he can get along on grass if you only woik him once in a while. But if you woik him steady, you got to give him grain."

He didn't elaborate, because he saw we were men of intelligence and could fill in for ourselves. A real job, besides calling for minimal qualifications that the broke man may not have, demands presentable clothes, a car that will get him to work, money on which to eat in restaurants at noon.

"It's better to get a hundred little jobs for a hundred little fellows dan one big job for one big fella, because den you got a hundred you can count on to work for ya, instead of one dat might likely cut your troat in da bargain," Brother Larry said.

I realized that New Orleans might be exotic in some respects but that in others it was exactly like everyplace else.

"How is it Jim always wins?" I asked, just to make conversation. "Because he works so hard?"

It was here, I think, that Brother Larry got the idea he had overrated me.

"If you watch da way elections goes," he said, "you will notice it's very seldom da Assessor gets beat."

Tom had neglected to tell me that Jim Comiskey's sole public office was Assessor of Taxes for the Eighth District of New Orleans, which includes most of the big buildings. He tells the property owners what they have to pay.

"I'll tell him you're coming to confession," Brother Larry yelled after us as we departed.

Early that Wednesday evening we drove down to the Third

Ward to sit in with Brother Jim, going through ghostly streets
of one- and two-story white clapboard houses out-at-elbow to
out-at-elbow, the obscurity broken only by the bright sign of
an occasional fried-chicken shack or one-story saloon. There
was no scent of magnolias, there were no lacy wrought-iron
balconies here. It was like a cross between Paterson, N.J., and
Port-au-Prince, and at night, with the crepe myrtles and the
scraggly palms invisible, there was nothing specifically southern. The insubstantiality of the buildings could be duplicated
in any run-down summer resort in the North. Here people
lived in them all year round, in the winter when they would
not be warm enough, and in the summer when any house at
all was too hot.

Jim Comiskey's headquarters was a one-story clapboard
building with a store front. Inside, there was a web of junk
around the walls: ladders, lathes, Coke bottles, paint cans,
ruptured Venetian blinds, tangles of electric wires, a water
cooler, a clothesline with clothespins and wire coat hangers,
all these objects except the clothesline looking as if they had
been simply kicked against the walls to clear a space in the
middle of the room. The clothesline was a *vestiaire* in winter,
when Comiskey's petitioners might have coats, but provision-
ally a torn cotton wrapper hung on it to dry.

Down the middle of the room there were two sections of
undertakers' chairs, one block occupied by a score or so of
dejected white men and the other by a lone Negro. At the
head of the room was an iron stove complete with pipe and
an ancient golden-oak writing desk. Back of it was a foul
toilet with a sheet hanging in front of it instead of a door,
and behind the desk sat Mr. Comiskey, a tall man, pink-faced,

blue-eyed, white-haired, benevolent of expression and dressed in sober but costly black shantung. He had the face of a popular cardinal, and looking at him, I was sure that if he had felt the vocation when young, he would be one by this time.

After he had disposed of the petitioner who was at his desk when we entered, a limpy man carrying an old straw hat, Tom and I approached the seat of power. My friend, who knew Comiskey of old, introduced me. He said I was a New Yorker interested in Louisiana politics, and that as such I couldn't afford to pass up the leader of the Old Regulars. Mr. Comiskey clasped my hand and looked into my eyes with two of honest blue. He called for chairs for us, and we sat down, like visitors to a class in session.

"They'll all have their turn," said the Assessor, with a wave of his hand toward the clients. "Everybody in the ward that have any trouble is here, and if they don't be here, they should be here. And anybody in Noo Wawlins is welcome. They all have somebody that they want to get into a hospital, or a job working for the Levee Board, or things of that nature and so forth. When I hear what they want, if it can be done, I process it to its final completion."

I could have closed my eyes and believed myself in Alderman Paddy Bauler's saloon in Chicago. There is neither Blue nor Gray when you get down to the American essentials.

I said gently that I had come to talk politics, and asked him what he had heard about Governor Long's condition, which was the *sine qua non* of the battle in the offing.

"I hear he's on da steady improve all da time," the Assessor said. "Fellas wit him at Hot Springs tell me he's champin' at da bit to go." He laughed happily. "He's like a hoss dat woik

is what he needs! He'll get better as he goes along. He's a
stoiling campaigner and as Governor he's doin' a wonderful
outstanding job."

"But don't you think this trouble with his wife will hurt
him?" I asked.

"I can't see wherein it will," he said. "Da women know da
Governor. He stops to talk to even kids, and he's coyteous wit
everybody. He sent Mrs. Comiskey a basket of cantaloupes
from Texas."

"Did he pay the express charges?"

"To be bruttally frank," the Assessor said, "he forgot. I had
to pay two dollars and seventy-six cents, and Mrs. Comiskey
says she could get da same cantaloupes for two dollars a dozen
at da market. But it shows how kind he is—always remembering his friends.

"You can't never count a Long out," he reminded me.
"Look at da form: Morrison and Dodd are past losers. Dey
have been at da post before and found lacking. You can't
never tell what will happen, but if he run back to form,
Earl got to win it all."

This was a degree of conviction I had not yet encountered
anywhere, and I felt a bit guilty in even asking Mr. Comiskey
whether he had heard talk about the Governor's income-tax
trouble. But relying on his realism, I asked just the same.

"To be bruttally frank," he said, "if he has income-tax
troubles possibly it might do him a lot of good wit de electorate. So many people are in da same boat dat dey might say,
'I hope him good luck!' If dey all vote for him, he's home
free."

Becoming slightly more serious, he said, "You got to realize dat when somebody slips Earl money it isn't for just his personal campaign. He uses it for candidates all over da state. He needs friends. Da Governor is an enforceful man. Like last fall, we had a young fella named McGovern over in St. Bernards we thought could make state senator if he had another fifty-five hundred dollars for his campaign. I call Earl one night and he calls me back next morning: 'Come up and get da green stuff.' No ifs and buts about Earl—no *mañana*."

Comiskey's words laid open for me a plan of defense in depth that might worry any Federal man.

With friends like him, I thought, old Earl would win it all.

CHAPTER **IV**

RACE AND OIL

Pausing for another cup of coffee in Thompson's Cafeteria on St. Charles on our way back from Comiskey's confessional, we heard a bit of news about the Third Force. Our acquaintance, the success from the Irish Channel, was having elevenses of apple pie à la mode and Coca-Cola. In New Orleans elevenses are P.M. and serve to fortify for the long night ahead. He was, as he had told us, a neo-Longite, but was always ready to jump to a winner. He viewed the political scene with the dispassionate glee of a horseplayer looking at the past-performance charts in the *Morning Telegraph*—entranced by the whole business, but not letting himself be swayed by affection for any particular horse.

"Perez is making his real play with Davis," he said when we had brought our coffee to his table. "He's throwing Willie Rainach to the alligators. Officially he'll be with Willie to start, but the deal's all set."

Already, although I had been in the Gret Stet only a few days, I could comprehend this jargon.

Leander Perez, the Pasha of Plaquemines Parish, was the Gret Stet's most powerful voice for the political sterilization of the Negro. ("Don't register your Negroes," a Governor named McEnery said in the nineties, "but don't forget to vote them.") He was also, even I knew, a racist of the obsessive kind often bred in regions of old admixture. Plaquemines is a coastal parish, once chiefly inhabited by muskrats, which now has more mineral wealth than any other in the state.

"A race of mixed blood, the product of various Latin progenitors, live on the islands and along the coast of the Gulf, who are termed Dagos," a political reporter named A. M. Gibson wrote of Louisiana at the end of the Civil War. "They are fruiters and fishermen. For a few dollars many of them can be hired to wield the assassin's knife." Whether all these violent men of "mixed blood" meekly accepted Negro status after 1876 is one of the small puzzles of Louisiana history, like the fate of that considerable society of cultured, ivory-tinted "colored" men and women, set free and enriched by their white fathers and grandfathers long before the Civil War, who excited J. W. De Forest's admiration when he came to New Orleans as a Union officer. (De Forest's outsider's impressions of New Orleans are one of the glories of a great war book, *A Volunteer's Adventures*. A third riddle of Louisianian history is what happened to the descendants of the soldiers in the Louisiana regiments of the *Union* Army. De Forest mentions several and tells especially of a brave charge of the First Louisiana infantry in the assault on Port Hudson. Its soldiers must have been sterile, like mules, for they left no visible descendants in their home state—either that or their offspring went underground and posed as Sons and Daughters of the Confederacy.)

It was therefore natural that Perez should support the campaign for Governor of pale, gloomy Willie Rainach, the state senator with a Confederate flag on his tie. Rainach, as chairman of a joint committee of the State Legislature on segregation, had made a spectacle of himself, and an enemy of Long, by prancing through the state purging "irregularly registered" colored voters from the rolls. In Iberville Parish, for example, the committee struck out the names of Negroes who, in the space marked "Color," had written "Negro" instead of "Black."

But though racism is a Perez obsession, sulphur, oil and gas are the revenues on which he feeds, and "local autonomy" is what he needs to preserve his domination.

"OIL and gas and sulphur! a magic combination of wealth for a parish and its people!" said an institutional ad I read in the *Times-Picayune* special supplement celebrating the centennial of the discovery of petroleum in America. "Plaquemines Parish produces more than twice as much oil yearly as any other Louisiana parish. It produces a great part of the world's urgently needed sulphur. And its gas reserves promise a bright future as the many miles of gas lines now under construction are connected with 'through pipe lines' serving the state and the nation. . . .

"SAID Judge Perez: 'We seek here to continue the traditional American way of life: freedom of enterprise, local control of our local destinies, high American standards of living.' "

With all that OIL, not to mention the gas and sulphur, he could afford the whim of staking a losing candidate in the preliminary heat, for the sake of his race hobby, but he must have a winner in the runoff to protect Plaquemines against investigation or legislation threatening "local control of local industries." The exploiting companies, no matter how mighty in Wall Street or Washington, are his captives in Plaquemines, as they used to be old Gomez's in Venezuela.

This time, our lawyer friend was telling us, Perez had decided to place his main bet on Jimmie Davis. The favorite, if he got to the post and did not break down, was Old Earl, but his condition was doubtful, and he was a declared personal enemy.

The second favorite on form was Chep Morrison. Long and Morrison were antitheses in all respects but one: they agreed on a sensible, calm approach to the color problem. This kept Louisiana agreeably free of the storms in neighboring states but made it hard for Perez to stomach either of them. Each of the two proclaimed himself a "thousand per cent," or occasionally a "million per cent," segregationist, but enemies accused both of being "soft on the niggers." School integration was not an immediate issue in the state, and neither was stirring it up. Both favored keeping Negroes on the registration rolls and giving them a fair share of social benefits. Naturally, both ran strong in colored election precincts.

The third man, Davis, was like a poker hand, open at both ends, ready to catch anything. He wanted the Negro vote *and* Perez's money.

Unfortunately, though, when you accept a man's support

you sometimes have to accept his quarrels, and our lawyer friend said: "Davis people saying as little as possible until after the first primary, because if Davis known as old Leander's man, it will hurt him with the nigger vote. The Morrison and Long people going to spread the news with the jigs as fast as they can."

The lawyer, a big man, went up to the counter for a second piece of pie à la mode. When he returned, he said with relish, "Upstate the Rainach people say they got a photograph of Davis dancing with Lena Horne at a theatrical party up north, and they going to spread it all over the state. So the niggers will cut him because he's Perez's man, and the redbones will down him for a nigger-lover."

It was the kind of paradox a politician could enjoy.

"Still, a lot of money's going there," he said. "Don't sell Davis short."

The lawyer demolished half his apple pie in a stroke and a gulp and then said, "Leander has things exactly his own way over in Plaquemines, and he wants it that way in the whole state. They're saying Davis has promised to change the name of the state flower for him if he's elected."

"What the hell's the use of that?" I asked innocently.

"From the Magnolia to the O-Leander," the lawyer explained, and he guffawed.

"He's the permanent District Attorney here," he said, "and appoints all the commissions. If you're an oil company and he don't like you, the safety commissioner will find a fire hazard so your rigs can't operate, and the highway commissioner will find your rigs are too heavy for the public roads so you can't move them. A couple of years ago when a union struck a friendly shipyard there, he arrested all the pickets on a charge of littering the public highway—they were smoking and throwing away the butts. It's an oil sheikdom, plus sulphur, and he's the sheik.

"You go over there to look up a title on land for a client that's an outsider and has a suit against an insider, and you find old books of deeds handwritten on parchment dating back to the seventeenth century. But when you come to the page about the land in dispute, it's typewritten on brand-new paper. You ask the parish clerk what happened, and he says, "Cockroaches ate the old page so bad we had to copy it out and replace it." His admiration was as pronounced as his taste for pie à la mode.

"Plaquemines has so many islands and trappers and fishermen lost up bayous, that's the excuse, that it's always the last parish in the state to come in with its vote, and that gives Leander a tactical advantage, y'unnerstand—a few hundred votes can make a big difference in a close race for Congress or the State Supreme Court. We elect Supreme Court justices down here one from each of seven districts.

"He hasn't enough votes to change Governor much—he has only about 15,000 people living there, and he can't report that many votes, because you gotta allow for a couple of children here and there. But it's the oil that counts—it gives him leverage."

This, I knew, was true. In its passion for politics, the Gret Stet of Loosiana, as southern Louisianians refer to it, resembles most closely the Arab republic of Lebanon, but in its economy it is closer akin to the Arab sheikdoms of the Persian Gulf. The Gret Stet floats on oil, like a drunkard's teeth on whiskey.

"Oil is to Louisiana what money is to a roulette game," Tom said. "It's what makes the wheel go round. It's the reason there are so many big bank rolls available to stake any politician who has a Formosa Chinaman's chance to get into office." Louisianians who make money in oil buy politicians, or pieces of politicians, as Kentuckians in the same happy situation buy race horses. Oil gets into politics, and politicians, making money in office, get into oil. The state slithers around in it.

"Louisiana is now the second biggest oil-and-gas-producing state in the country, after Texas," Tom went on. "The state gets an average of twenty-five cents in severance tax on every barrel of oil released from the earth, and last year the output ran to over eight hundred thousand barrels a day, which amounted to a take of around seventy million dollars. The state also puts an ad-valorem tax on all the real property of the industry. That's ten million more, and then there's all the millions for leases on state-owned oil land, inshore and offshore. We're in a class with Bahrein and Kuwait. This is a rich state full of poor people, just like those Arab sheikdoms. Ten years ago, Louisiana ranked thirty-ninth among the states in per-capita income, and it's probably not much higher now. But where the state differs from the Persian Gulf is that here the natives vote. The hardest fight Huey Long had was to put the severance tax on oil, but now no politician would dare talk of taking it off. It's the same with the pensions that the oil tax pays. Eighty per cent of the people over sixty-five in the state are on that blessed pension. Seventy-two dollars a month. And they aren't the only ones who benefit. They've all got children and grandchildren, who'd have to support them otherwise."

"Some of the money sifts through to the parishes, too, hear?" the lawyer said. "The parish in which the oil is located gets a share of the state's share to use on roads and schools. When it's a parish with a lot of oil and a small population, that give the local boss a mighty fine jackpot to cut."

Politics in Vermont might wheel more freely, too, if the home folks knew the state was floating on an oil field.

It is impossible for a candidate to run without oil money. As in Lebanon, campaigning in Louisiana presents a high per-capita voter cost. But, since the oil men are competitive, they place their principal stakes on competing candidates, with "savers" on others and a certain amount of around-the-table baksheesh even to their sworn enemies, to turn away wrath in case the worst happens.

The oil has worked deep into the pores of the state; only five parishes out of sixty-four have no producing wells. Of these, one, Orleans, consists of the city of New Orleans, and there may be oil under that too. Politics has been a passion of Louisianians since the eighteenth century, however. Oil is an addendum. Now they are inextricably mixed.

The aleatory nature of the oil business facilitates the mixing. A safe way to pay a man a bribe is to buy a bit of worthless swamp from him for a high price, as "potential oil land." To buy it simply as real estate would appear too raw. Another method is to let him in at a low price on a well that is about to prove up.

The mysterious oil business is also a perfect instrument for decontaminating hot money; a gambler or a rackets man with a large accumulation of unreported profit buys a modest well, which immediately becomes, on his tax returns, fabulously productive. He pays tax on part of his hoard—at the lenient rates prescribed for oil men—and thereby legitimizes the rest.

If all oil men were content to remain such, except for harmless hobbies like raising prize cattle and keeping women, their effect on politics in the Gret Stet might be no worse than that of silver dollars on slot machines. Unfortunately, some of them have political ideas, an insight I acquired while lunching magnificently with two hospitable New Orleans brothers, a Republican and a Democrat. The Republican was a big man. The Democrat was the size of a grand champion Clydesdale horse, nineteen hands at the shoulder. Like all Louisiana Republicans in good times, the Republican brother was an important Federal official; the Democratic mammoth, I soon gathered, had of late years been lucky in his oil gambles. The Republican took a detached but appreciative view of the situation. The Democrat said that he liked Willie Rainach.

"He's just a country boy," the Republican brother said.

"He's a country gentleman," Big Man answered.

"My brother has more money than political sense," said the Republican.

It was evident that they had argued Rainach often, but they dropped the argument there and bore me off to Manale's, a restaurant with the aspect of a saloon, far from the French Quarter, where they provided a glorious lunch of pompanos studded with busters—fat soft-shell crabs shorn of their limbs, which are to the buster-fancier as trifling as a mustache on the *plat du jour* must seem to a cannibal. Driving me to my hotel, Big Man, the genial and solicitous host, called my attention to a pert redheaded girl walking along the street and flirting her tail in the attractive Southern manner.

"See her?" he said. "Passing for white. She's a nigger." And his good-humored double truck of a face was red with fury.

Under a state administration with Leander Perez's approval, I knew such anomalies would be rectified on a subjective basis. The registrar of births of a Louisiana parish has the right to change the status of parents retroactively by marking their child's birth certificate "colored." In such cases "common report" and the registrar's opinion of the physical appearance of child and parents govern. The registrar, usually a woman, is legally presumed to know "who is who."

The parents of a child thus ruled "colored" automatically, under law, become colored people too, or if the registrar impugns only one of them they are guilty of miscegenation, a serious crime. Challenges are usually based on gossip, malice, "intuition" or a combination of any two or all.

The parents may sue to force the registrar to change her decision, but the burden of proof is then upon them to demonstrate that all the ancestors of both for five generations back were white, a task that would tax any white person anywhere. (Name your thirty-two great-great-grandparents. Find a natal document for each, or, failing that, what was "common report.") Only the brave and relatively rich can undertake such litigation, and only a Pudd'nhead Wilson of a lawyer can win a color case. Under nonfictional conditions, Pudd'nhead Wilsons come high.

Tom, a believer in the visual approach to teaching, said that I needed a glimpse, no matter how brief, of the oil and gas business. (There was little to be gained by further palaver in New Orleans; we had reached the stage when we were beginning to pick up rumors that we ourselves had started.)

"Let's go down and look at a drilling barge tomorrow," he said.

We drove across the bridge over the Mississippi and south along the west bank to a point about twenty miles below the city, in the parish of Plaquemines. There was warm rain all the way. We drove down a side road toward the river and left my guide's station wagon in front of a cluster of Negro shanties huddling under the levee. Then we walked a slithery path along the edge of the levee to a point where we saw a catwalk out to a plank boat landing. The drilling barge lay, or stood, about one hundred yards out in the stream, a creature at once reminiscent of a giant sucking insect, a birthday cake with nine candles, and the skyline of a factory city. It was a great platform, resting on the water's surface, with the superstructure of an oil well rising from its center and eight tall shafts, like factory chimneys, towering toward the sky around its perimeter.

These shafts, called jacks, are the barge's feet. When she arrives in working position she thrusts down the lower extremities of the great rods until they dig into the sea bottom and hold her fast. She then rises on them, like an automobile on jacks, until there is a good clearance between her bottom and sea level. From a seagoing vessel she has changed to a house on stilts.

Next she extrudes from her belly the business end of the drill that she will thrust ten or fifteen thousand feet beneath the bed of gulf or ocean until she reaches oil or gas—or the charterer gives up. Then she lowers herself to the surface of the water, retracts her under parts into her hull and is ready to be towed to her next job. There is so much machinery within her hull that there is no room for an organ of locomotion.

She is a specialized succubus, a great pipette, moved about to wherever her manipulators think there may be blood worth sucking. Such a barge may work for her owner, if he has leased new undersea acreage, or, which is more common, she may be chartered to companies that have acreage and no barge. This one, Sancton said, was new and had cost four and a half million dollars to build.

She weighed four thousand dead-weight tons, as much as a fair-sized tramp steamer, and contained, in addition to the mechanisms of her gymnastic and oil-searching systems, a plant for distilling sea water for hydraulic drilling. Tom said the barge in the river in front of us was called the *Mr. Louie*, after her owner, promoter and chief conceiver, a man named Louis Roussel.

We walked out onto the catwalk and shouted and waved our arms at the barge's tender, an old LCT, or landing-craft tank, with long forward deck and a high pilot house at her stern. The LCT lay under the monster's quarter, swinging lazy at her cable. A workman on the *Mr. Louie* cast the line off and the old warrior turned toward shore and came in through the muddy water. Her one-man crew, a big mulatto bare to the waist, brought her alongside the plank and held her there by her own power as we stepped aboard, then backed her out and wheeled her under the barge. A crane man in the high superstructure lowered a rope basket cage at the end of a cable to the LCT's deck. We stepped inside and grabbed hold, and he swung us up in the air like a couple of crabs in a long-handled net, then brought us inboard and set us gently down.

From the steaming 100-degree heat of the deck, we walked through a door into an air-conditioned mess hall as cold as an iced drink. Two men in coveralls were seated at a long plastic-topped steel table drinking Cokes. One was the owner, Roussel. He explained that with one of the other men, his naval architect, he had been running final trials of his creation's jacking system.

"She can work in a hundred and twenty feet of water," he said. "When she's set she's as solid as an island. She'll carry a working crew of eleven, living in air-conditioned quarters, with unlimited fresh water, twenty feet above the surface of the sea, if it's rough."

I asked him, not unnaturally, how the owner or lessee of such an elaborate tool chose a place to use it.

"You go out in a boat," he said, pronouncing boat "bawat," with two syllables, in the Cajun way, "and you try a seismic shot." (The shot is a charge of dynamite detonated under water.) "The best way I can explain it is that the vibrations are like a rubber ball. If the ball bounces hard enough, you know it has hit something solid. You measure the bounce of the shot by its vibrations. If they show you are over what we call a dome, or salt dome, formation, there's a chance that there's oil under it. Naturally, if you're near a field that's already producing, you have a better chance. But everybody has the same idea—the area will have a higher selling price. If you're away from the rest, using your own judgment, you're wildcatting, but you get better odds if you're right."

I realized that he was describing a process necessarily complex, but he made it sound simple.

"And then, if you decide you want to drill?" I asked.

"You make a map showing what you want," he said. "That's called a lot, and it can't be more than five thousand eight hundred acres. You send a deposit of one hundred dollars to the State Minerals Board with a letter saying you want to bid on that lot. The Board calls for bids on the lot by a certain date. Then, if you bid high enough, you get the lease."

"How many acres are there altogether?"

"Quite a few, I imagine," he said. "The whole coast from Texas to Mississippi, out to a distance of ten and a half miles from the land. You know about the dispute between the Federal Government and the state, probably. The State Minerals Board runs the show meanwhile, and the money paid for leases is held in escrow." (The United States Supreme Court has since ruled against Louisiana, but Congress may bail the Gret Stet out.)

Square-chinned and leathery, Roussel has the kind of head Norman peasants carve on wooden stoppers for Calvados bottles.

From their respective inceptions, Texas and Oklahoma have had a frontier character. Oil men there, or so it seems to me, are primarily oil men. But Louisiana is a very old com-

munity, for America, and the independents in oil are varied
and indigenous types: Roussel, for example, said he had been
a bus driver in New Orleans in 1930. He had made a bit of
money and bought a share in a wildcat drilling venture. The
well had come in, and he had gone on venturing, like a man
with the dice in his hand. He had not had to move far to get
from his bus route to his holes; he was as native as a muskrat,
as French as his taste for litigation. He had backed five successive winners, which is as hard as five successive passes.
Then he had drilled "a big one I won't brag about, because
it was dry."

If he had had the bad luck first, he might still be driving a
bus. But by that time he was out ahead, like a crap shooter with
a big bankroll.

CHAPTER **V**

NOTHING BUT A LITTLE PISSANT

The entry of a hero on the public scene goes unnoticed, but his *rentrée* always has an eager press. Napoleon coming back from Elba, Robert Bruce from rustication among the spiders, and Jim Jeffries from retirement in 1910, all drew a heavy coverage; so, no doubt, did Odysseus after he announced his arrival at Ithaca. The betting public, sentimental only to a point, wants to know whether the hero's legs are sound, his spirits good, whether he has shed the lard of sloth, and if so, whether he has weakened himself taking off weight.

Such was the mood of Louisiana when, on the afternoon of August 2, Tom and I started from New Orleans in his battered station wagon to go to the midstate city of Alexandria, where Earl was to make the first major stump speech of his campaign for renomination on the Democratic ticket.

Opinion, all biased, was split on how the Governor would shape up. The *Times-Picayune,* like the Royalist journals in 1815, held that the man from Elba was a burned-out shadow of a hollow shell. But Jim Comiskey, boss of the Old Regulars, had assured me "Oil is on da steady improve and champing on da bit to go." Mister Comiskey was, for the moment, a red-hot Long man.

Tom was about as neutral as a Louisianian can be during a primary fight, which is to say about as calm as a cat can stay with catnip under its nose. He erred, however, in overweighting medical testimony. This is a mistake journalists have made increasingly since 1953, when, after President Eisenhower's heart attack, the statements of physicians in attendance became more newsworthy than good triangle murders. Abruptly, any utterance of an M.D. rated as much space as the award of an honorary degree to the pubisher of the paper, and editors, not content with the daily bulletins from Denver, Washington and Harvard, sent reporters out to ask local cardiologists everywhere for inside comments on the Chief Executive's viscera. These covered everything from the effect of fried mush to how many times a day a middle-aged man ought to lose his temper. Reporters, always confused between what is news and what makes sense, began to take the doctors seriously. After that the cholesterol was in the fire.

Tom was impressed because half the doctors in the South and Southwest had tabbed Uncle Earl as infected with all known diseases, from paranoid schizophrenia to warts and bronchiectasis, which means difficulty in clearing the throat. Even his own experts, who denied he was demented, said in explanation of his antislavery views that he was beset by arteriosclerosis, several small strokes, oscillatory blood pressure and an irreverent gleam in his left eye. The collective diagnosis recalled the doctor described in the great book

The Flush Times in Alabama and Mississippi, who would "fire at random a box of his pills into your bowels, with a vague chance of hitting some disease unknown to him." It was Tom who, years before, had first called my attention to the *Flush Times,* by Joseph G. Baldwin, a happy 1853 antidote to the mystic-memories-of-magnolia school of Southern writing.

"There is an expert at Tulane they call 'Dr. Schizophrenia,'" Tom said to me. "He says Earl hasn't got it. But what he says he has is progressive deterioration of the memory caused by an occluded ventricle. Once they got that, they're gone."

I myself inclined to the theory that if a man knows enough to go to the races, he needs no doctor. A good tout is the best physician for a confirmed horseplayer, and any prescription he writes that pays 5 to 1 or better tonifies the blood, synchronizes the pulse, regularizes the functions and lets bygones be bygones.

The distance from New Orleans to Alexandria is about 190 miles. The first 90 miles, from New Orleans to Baton Rouge, are on a throughway, a straight, fast road on the east side of the Mississippi, far enough back from the bank to avoid meanders, and high enough over the marshes to obviate bridges. There is nothing worth a long look. The bayous parallel the road on either side like stagnant, weed-strangled ditches, but their life is discreetly subsurface—snapping turtles, garfish, water moccasins and alligators. The mammals are water rats and muskrats and nutria, a third kind of rat. The nutria, particularly ferocious, is expropriating the other rats. Bird life, on the day we drove through, was a patrol of turkey buzzards looking down for rat cadavers. There pressed down on the landscape a smell like water that householders have inadvertently left flowers in while they went off for a summer holiday. It was an ideal setting for talk about politics.

The old station wagon slammed along like an old selling plater that knows a course by heart.

"It's the most complex state in the South," my companion said. "In just about every one of the others you have the same battle between the poor-to-middling farmers on the poor lands—generally in the hills—that didn't justify an investment in slaves before the war, and the descendants of the rich planters on the rich lands, who held slaves by the dozen to the gross. Slaves were a mighty expensive form of agricultural machinery, with a high rate of depreciation. You could only use them to advantage on land that produced a cash crop. We had that same basic conflict, and it lasted longer than anywhere else, for reasons I'm going to give, but in addition, we have a lot that are all our own. In the other states it was just between poor Anglo-Saxon Protestant whites and rich Anglo-Saxon Protestant whites. But here we got poor French Catholic whites and poor Anglo-Saxon whites and rich French Catholic whites and rich Anglo-Saxon Protestant whites. Sometimes the Catholic French get together against the Anglo-Saxon Protestants and sometimes the rich of both faiths get together against the poor, or the poor against the rich.

"And there's always been another problem in Louisiana that no other Southern state has. There are other large collections of people living close together in the South, but they are not big cities, just overgrown country towns like Atlanta. They may have corruption, but not sophistication. They lack the urban psychology, like ancient Athens, that is different, hostile, and superior, and that the countryman resents and distrusts. So you get a split along another line—you got not only poor rural French Catholic, rich rural white Protestant, rich rural French Catholic, and poor rural white Protestant, but poor urban Catholic, not exclusively French, rich urban Catholic, poor urban Protestant (mainly Negro) and rich urban Protestant. Making out a ticket is tricky.

"Alick, in Rapides Parish, is the political navel of the state, right in the middle." (Alick is Alexandria.) "Southern, bilingual, French Catholic Louisiana, the land of the bougalees, shades into Northern monolingual, Anglo-Saxon Protestant Louisiana, the land of the rednecks. But in Rapides itself and the parishes across the center of the state you get both kinds. So there's always a lot of politicking and name-calling in Alick, and when Earl picked it to stump in he showed he was ready to fight."

He sounded as complacent as a man I remembered on the road to Baalbek, telling me of the Ten Varieties soup of politico-religious divisions within the Lebanon.

The old car banged along. Its speedometer was not working, but it had a clock in its head, like an old horse that an old trainer, set in his ways, has worked a mile in 1.47 every Wednesday morning since it was three years old.

"Orleans Parish—that's the city of New Orleans—and Jefferson, across the river, which is its dormitory country—have about a quarter of a million voters between them," my instructor said. "That's between twenty-five and thirty per cent of the state vote. All the parishes north of a line through

Rapides have maybe twenty per cent and all the parishes south of it and west of the Mississippi maybe twenty to twenty-five. The central chunk, on an axis from Alick to Baton Rouge and on east, has the balance of strength. To get a majority of votes on the first primary, a candidate got to win big in one of the four regions and make it close in the others, or win big in three and lose big in one. They're so different and so opposed historically that it's hard to imagine a candidate running evenly in all four. Old Earl was so strong in 1956 that he ran *almost* even in the metropolis. For an upstate candidate that's great. He won easy everyplace else.

"If Earl is too sick to run, a Catholic from New Orleans like Morrison might win big in New Orleans and south Louisiana, but he would be snowed under in the north, and he would have to run like hell in Alick and Baton Rouge to make it. So probably there would be no winner the first time around, and then, in the runoff between the two high men, anything could happen. Generally all the losers gang up against the top guy. Hard to name a favorite in the betting until the day before the second runoff, and then often you're wrong anyway."

"Then how did Huey Long put all the bits and pieces together?" I asked.

"Huey got all the poor people over on one side," my friend said. "And there were a lot more of them. He made the poor redneck and the poor Frenchman and the poor Negro see that what they had in common was more important for voting purposes than the differences. The differences couldn't be changed by ballots. The Depression helped, of course.

"When people are living good again they can afford to

fight over unessentials. The regime that ran Louisiana right on from the Purchase discouraged the idea that a man had the right to live decently. It was new stuff down here when Huey put it out: 'Share Our Wealth'; 'Every Man a King'; and remember, he got to be Governor four years before Franklin D. Roosevelt was elected President. Huey got after the out-state oil companies and the in-state oil companies, and the old-family bench and bar that held with the out-state money, and anybody that gave him an argument for any reason he blackened with being a hireling of Standard Oil. I don't know how much money he made out of it, but certainly less than a lot of politicians make taking the easy money side.

"And whether he did it all because he loved the sense of power is moot—you could say the same thing against any leader you didn't like. I think up North you got the idea that the man who killed him became a popular hero, like William Tell or Charlotte Corday. Incidentally, Charlotte Corday wouldn't have won any Gallup polls in Paris in her day. There were editorials that said, 'Louisiana heaved a sigh of relief and raised her tear-stained head from the dust.'

"But, in fact, Dick Leche and Earl Long, who ran for Governor and Lieutenant Governor on the Long ticket in 1936, got sixty-seven and a tenth per cent of the popular vote, even though there was a fight among the Long people themselves and Leche was next to unknown then. That was a better percentage than even Roosevelt got against Landon that year. The vote came straight from the tear-stained head."

We got hungry and stopped at a glass-and-Monel-metal hangar that advertised "Shrimp, BarBQue, PoBoy" (this last

the Louisiana term for what we call Italian hero sandwiches).
The BarBQue was out, the shrimps stiff with inedible batter,
the coffee desperate. Southern cooking, outside New Orleans,
is just about where Frederick Law Olmsted left it when he
wrote *The Cotton Kingdom*. A PoBoy at Mumphrie's in New
Orleans is a portable banquet. In the South proper, it is a
crippling blow to the intestine.

"We're hitting a new culture belt," I said. "This is the
kind of cooking that goes right on up the center of the United
States with the Mississippi until it hits the Great Lakes. It's
nearer akin to what we'd get in a roadside diner in La
Grange, Illinois, than to the poorest oyster bar in New
Orleans, sixty miles behind us."

Tom, New Orleans born, of parents born there, said,
"You're right on that. We're Mediterranean. I've never been
to Greece or Italy, but I'm sure I'd be at home there as soon
as I landed."

He would, too, I thought. New Orleans resembles Genoa
or Marseilles, or Beirut or the Egyptian Alexandria more
than it does New York, although all seaports resemble one
another more than they can resemble any place in the interior. Like Havana and Port-au-Prince, New Orleans is
within the orbit of a Hellenistic world that never touched
the North Atlantic. The Mediterranean, Caribbean and Gulf
of Mexico form a homogeneous, though interrupted, sea.
New York and Cherbourg and Bergen are in a separate thalassic system.

Hellenism followed the Mediterranean littoral; it spread
to the shores of the Caribbean and Gulf. The Hellenistic
world stopped short of the Atlantic edge of Europe, but its

Roman conquerors got there with a version in *Reader's Digest* form, like Irish missionaries of a Jewish religion. Culture on both shores of the North Atlantic is therefore a paraphrase, as if Choctaws had learned English from Cherokees.

The Mediterraneans who settled the shores of the interrupted sea scurried across the gap between the Azores and Puerto Rico like a woman crossing a drafty hall in a sheer nightgown to get to a warm bed with a man in it. Old, they carried with them a culture that had ripened properly, on the tree. Being sensible people, they never went far inland. All, or almost all, the interior of North America was therefore filled in from the North Atlantic Coast, by the weakest element in that incompletely civilized population—those who would move away from salt water.

The middle of Louisiana is where the culture of one great thalassic littoral impinges on the other, and a fellow running for Governor has got to straddle the line between them.

When Tom and I were sufficiently disgusted with the coffee of the inland-dwellers, we resumed our ride, bypassing the center of Baton Rouge to cross the Mississippi by the Baton Rouge bridge, and after that leaving the monotony of the throughway for the state roads with their complete lack of variety. By now I had begun to sneak compulsive glances at my watch. We had left New Orleans at four, and Earl was slated to speak at eight. The owner of the old station wagon had said he could make it to Alick in four hours easy. It began to look not all that easy.

I tried to estimate the station wagon's speed by clocking it between signposts. From "Bunkie, 27 Mi." To "Bunkie, 20

Mi.," I caught it in a consoling seven minutes, but the next post, a good bit farther on, said "Bunkie, 23." Bunkie is the leading bourgade between Baton Rouge and Alick—it has a population of 4,666—but there were other one-street-of-storefronts towns that the road ran through. By now it was dusk and the stores were lighted, so that, coming out of the dark, we galloped episodically between plywood maple-finished bedroom suites in the windows on one side of the street and mannequins with $7.98 dresses on the other, scaring from our course gaunt hounds that looked like Kabyle dogs.

The entrance to Alick was little more impressive than these others, except for two electric signs. One was a straw-hatted spook flapping great wings over the Hocus-Pocus Liquor Store and the other a symbolic giraffe and dachshund over a used-car lot. They disappeared at every other flash in favor of a legend: "High Quality, Low Prices."

Hurrying through otherwise undistinguished streets, we passed between cars parked thick along the approaches to the courthouse square and heard the loud-speaker blaring long before we got there. Somebody was on the platform in front of the courthouse steps, standing too close to the micro-phone and blasting. The crowd, massed immediately around the speaker's stand, thinned out toward the sidewalks.

My companion let me out and drove on to find a parking space, and I ran onto the lawn for my first look at the Imam in the flesh. As I crossed over to the forum, a boy handed me a pink throwaway, which I examined when I got within range of the light diffused from the floodlamps over the platform:

Governor Long Opens Campaign for Re-Election

Come Out and Bring All your friends to hear the truth. Come out and see Governor Long in person. Nothing will be said to offend or hurt anyone.

The Governor, on the platform, was saying to somebody I could not see over in the other wing of the audience:

"If you don't shut up your claptrap, I'm going to have you forcibly removed. You just nothing but a common hoodlum and a heckler."

"Amen," an old man in front of me yelled. "Give it to him, Earl."

Whoever it was that Earl was talking to in the crowd had no microphone, so we couldn't hear him, but he must have answered in tones audible to the Governor, because the latter shouted into the mike:

"I knew your daddy, Camille Gravel, and he was a fine man. But you trying to make yourself a big man, and you nothing but a little pissant."

"Amen, Earl," the old man yelled. "Give it to him."

The fellow in the crowd, now identified for me as a lawyer from Alick who was the Democratic National Committeeman from Louisiana, must have spoken again, for the Governor thundered:

"Mr. Gravel, I got nothing against you personally. Now you keep quiet and I won't mention your name. If you don't I'll have you removed as a common damn nuisance." He paused for the answer we couldn't hear and then bellowed:

"If *you* so popular, why don't *you* run for Governor?"

It sounded like a dialogue between a man with the horrors and his hallucinations. But the National Committeeman, Earl's interlocutor, was there in the flesh. He had brought his ten children, and they were all mad at the Governor.

The night was like a heavy blanket pressed down on the lawn. Men stood in their sleeveless, collarless shirts, and sweat caked the talcum powder on the backs of the women's necks. Anti-Long newspapers the next day conceded the crowd was between three and four thousand, so there may well have been more. Plenty of Negroes, always in little groups, were scattered among the whites, an example, I suppose, of Harry Golden's "vertical integration," because in public gatherings where there are seats, the two colors are always separated into blocs.

"That's the way I like to see it," the Governor said, from the stand. "Not all our colored friends in one spot and white friends in another. I'm the best friend the poor white man, and the middle-class white man, and the rich white man—so long as he behave himself—and the poor colored man, ever had in the State of Loosiana. And if the NAACP and that little pea-headed nut Willie Rainach will just leave us alone, then *sen*sible people, not cranks, can get along in a *reas*onable way. That Rainach wants to fight the Civil War all over again."

There were two colored couples, middle-aged, in front of me, next to the old white man who didn't like Gravel, and now one of the colored men shouted "Amen!" The old white man gave him a reproving look, but he couldn't bawl him out for agreeing with a Long. Nobody can object to *reas*onable and *sen*sible, but Long hadn't said what he thought *reas*onable and *sen*sible were, and it occurred to me that he probably never would.

I had been looking at him with an amateur clinical eye since I got there, and his physical condition seemed to me to have improved several hundred per cent since his stump appearance with Joe Sims on the Fourth of July. Late hours and a diet of salted watermelon, buttermilk, and Vienna sausages cut up in chicken broth had put a dozen pounds back on his bones. Walking between grandstands and paddocks had legged him up, and he pranced under the floodlights that must have raised the temperature to a hundred and ten or so. I remembered when I had seen first the referee, Ruby Goldstein, and then the great Sugar Ray Robinson himself collapse under the heat of similar lights in a ring on a less oppressive night in New York.

Uncle Earl wore a jacket, shirt and tie, a pattern of statesmanlike conventionality on a night when everybody off the platform was coatless and tieless. The tie itself was a quiet pattern of inkblots against an olive-and-pearl background, perhaps a souvenir Rorschach test from Galveston. The suit, a black job that dated from the days when he was fat and sassy, hung loosely about him as once it had upon a peg in the supermarket where the Governor liked to buy his clothes.

He left the dude role to Morrison. And in fact, before the evening was over, he said:

"I see Dellasoups has been elected one of the ten best-dressed men in America. He has fifty-dollar neckties and four-hundred-dollar suits. A four-hundred-dollar suit on old Uncle Earl would look like socks on a rooster."

It is difficult to report a speech by Uncle Earl chronologically, listing the thoughts in order of appearance. They chased one another on and off the stage like characters in a Shakespearean battle scene, full of alarums and sorties. But Morrison, good roads and old-age pensions popped in quite often.

Of Dodd, the State Auditor, a quondam ally and now a declared rival for the Governorship, he said, "I hear Big Bad Bill Dodd has been talking about inefficiency and waste in this administration. Ohyeah. Ohyeah. Well let me tell you, Big Bad Bill has at least six streamlined deadheads on his payroll that couldn't even find Bill's office if they had to. But they can find that *Post Office* every month to get their salary check—Ohyeah."

It was after the *"reas*onable and *sens*ible" bit that he went into his general declaration of tolerance. "I'm not against anybody for reasons of race, creed, or any ism he might believe in except nuttism, skingameism or communism," he said.

"I'm glad to see so many of my fine Catholic friends here— they been so kind to me I sometimes say I consider myself forty per cent Catholic and sixty per cent Baptist" (this is a fairly accurate reflection of the composition of the electorate). "But I'm in favor of *every* religion with the possible exception of snake-chunking. Anybody that so presumes on how he stands with Providence that he will let a snake bite him, I say he deserves what he's got coming to him." The snake-chunkers, a small, fanatic cult, do not believe in voting.

"Amen, Earl," the old man said.

The expressions on the Governor's face changed with the poetry of his thought, now benign, now mischievous, now indignant. Only the moist hazel eyes remained the same, fixed on a spot above and to the rear of the audience as if expecting momentarily the arrival of a posse.

"I don't *need* this job," he said. "I don't *need* money." He stopped and winked. "I don't miss it except when I run out."

There were shouts of laughter, the effect he courted.

"Amen, Earl. You tell 'em, Earl."

His face turned serious, as if he had not expected to be so cruelly misunderstood.

"I'm serious about that," he said. You know I'm no goody-goody. But if I have ever misappropriated one cent, by abuse of my office, and anyone can prove it, I'll resign.

"I know lots of ways to make a living. I know how to be a lawyer, and a danged good one. I know how to be a traveling salesman. I know how to pick cotton, and have many times, although I've seen the days when to get my hundred pounds I had to put a watermelon in the bag."

There were gales of tolerant laughter now, even from farmers who would shoot any of their own help they found cheating on weight.

"All I ask," he said, with the honesty throbbing in his voice like a musical saw, "is a chance once again to help the fine people of the Great State of Loosiana, and to continue to serve them as their Governor."

Even a group of great louts in T shirts, perhaps high-school football players, were silent and by now impressed; earlier in the address they had made a few feeble attempts at heckling, like yelling, "Hey, Earl, what's in the glass?" when the Governor paused for a drink of water. These boys might be from well-to-do anti-Long families, but they had the endemic Southern (and Arabic) taste for oratory, and they knew a master when they heard him.

Mr. Gravel, down near the platform, must have again attracted the Governor's attention, but now Uncle Earl, the creature of his own voice, was in a benign mood from offering his own body to the Great State of Loosiana.

"Mr. Gravel," he said, "you got ten beautiful children there, I wish you would lend five of them to me to bring up." It was one of Earl's well-publicized sorrows that he, like the Shah of Iran then, had no legitimate heir, and he handed peppermint candies or small change to all children he saw, even in years when there was no election. "He bought those candies by grosses of dozens," an ex-associate told me.

Mr. Gravel, still inaudible except to Earl, must have declined this overture, because the Governor shouted to the crowd: "He used to be a nice fellow, but now he just a goddamn hoodlum!"

"Leave him alone, Earl, we come to hear *you* talk!" the old man near me shouted back.

"I was in Minneannapolis once, talking to the Governor of Minnesota, a great expert on insanity," Uncle Earl said, "and he told me an astonishing fact—there are ten times as many crazy people in Minnesota as Louisiana. I suppose that is on account of the cold climate. They cannot go around in their shirt sleeves all year around, go huntin' and fishin' in all seasons, as we do. We got a wonderful climate," he said, and paused to wipe the sweat from his face with a handkerchief soaked in Coca-Cola, which he poured from a bottle out of a bucket of ice handed him by one of the lesser candidates on his ticket. The bugs soaring up at the edge of the lighted area and converging on the floodlights formed a haze as thick as a beaded curtain.

"On account we got so few crazy people, we can afford to let Camille Gravel run around."

"Leave him up, Earl," the old man yelled. "You got him licked."

"Some sapsuckers talk about cutting down taxes," the Governor said, apropos of nothing he had been talking about. "Where are they going to start cutting expenses? On the *spastic* school?" (When any opponent suggests a cut in welfare expenditures, Earl accuses him of wanting to take it out on the spastics. This is the equivalent of charging the fellow would sell his mother for glue.) "They want to cut down on the *spastics?* On the little children, enjoying the school lunches? Or on those fine old people, white-haired against the sunset of life—" and he bowed his own white head for a split second—"who enjoy the most generous state pensions in the United States?

"We got the finest roads, finest schools, finest hospitals in the country—yet there are rich men who complain. They are so tight you can hear 'em squeak when they walk. They wouldn't give a nickel to see a earthquake. They sit there swallowin' hundred-dollar bills like a bullfrog swallows minners—if you chunked them as many as they want they'd bust."

"Amen, Earl," the old man said. "God have mercy on the poor people."

"Of course, I know many *fine* rich people," the Governor said, perhaps thinking of his campaign contributors. "But the most of them are like a rich old feller I knew down in

Plaquemines Parish, who died one night and never done nobody no good in his life, and yet, when the Devil come to get him, he took an appeal to St. Peter.

" 'I done some good things on earth,' he said. 'Once, on a cold day in about 1913, I gave a blind man a nickel.' St. Peter looked all through the records, and at last, on page four hundred and seventy-one, he found the entry. 'That ain't enough to make up for a misspent life,' he said. 'But wait,' the rich man says. 'Now I remember, in 1922 I give five cents to a poor widow woman that had no carfare.' St. Peter's clerk checked the book again, and on page thirteen hundred and seventy-one, after pages and pages of how this old stump-wormer loan-sharked the poor, he found the record of that nickel.

" 'That ain't neither enough,' St. Peter said. But the mean old thing yelled, *'Don't* sentence me yet. In about 1931 I give a nickel to the Red Cross.' The clerk found that entry, too. So he said to St. Peter, 'Your Honor, what are we going to do with him?' "

The crowd hung on Uncle Earl's lips the way the bugs hovered in the light.

"You know what St. Peter said?" the Governor, the only one in the courthouse square who knew the answer, asked. There was, naturally, no reply.

"He said: 'Give him back his fifteen cents and tell him to go to Hell.' "

He had the crowd with him now, and he dropped it.

"Folks," he said, "I know you didn't come here just to hear me talk. If this big mouth of mine ever shut up I'd be in a devil of a fix. I want to introduce to you some of the fine *sin*cere candidates that are running with me on my ticket. My ticket and the independent candidates I have endorsed are trained, skilled, and have the wisdom and experience to make you honest, loyal and *sin*cere public servants."

He turned to the triple row of men and women who sat behind him on undertaker's chairs, the men swabbing, the women dabbing, at their faces with handkerchiefs, while the Governor talked like an intrepid trainer who turns his back on his troupe of performing animals.

A reporter who had his watch on the Governor said that his talk had lasted fifty-seven minutes, and he was not even blowing.

"And first," he said, "I want to introduce to you the man I have selected to serve under me as Lieutenant Governor during my next term of office—a fine Frenchmun, a fine Catholic, the father of twenty-three children, Mr. Oscar Guidry."

The number of children was politically significant, since it indicated that Mr. Guidry was a practicing, not a *soi-disant,* Catholic. The candidate for Lieutenant Governor had to be a Frenchman and a Catholic, because Uncle Earl was neither.

Mr. Guidry, a short, stocky man who reminded me of a muscular owl, arose from his chair like a Mr. Bones called to front center by Mr. Interlocutor. He appeared embarrassed, and he whispered rapidly to Uncle Earl.

"Oscar says he has only fourteen children," the Governor announced. "But that's a good beginnin'."

Mr. Guidry whispered again, agitated, and Earl said, "But he is a member of a family of twenty-three brothers and sisters." He turned away, as if washing his hands of the whole affair, and sat down.

Mr. Guidry, throwing back his head and clasping his hands in front of him, as if about to intone the "Marseillaise," began with a rush, sounding all his aitches:

"I am *honored* to be associated with the Gret Governeur of the Gret Stet on his tiquette. Those who have conspired against him, fearing to shoot him with a pistol-ball . . ." and he was off, but Earl, seated directly behind him, was mugging and catching flies, monopolizing attention like an old vaudeville star cast in a play with a gang of Method actors.

Pulling his chair slightly out of line, he crossed his legs and turned his profile to the audience, first plucking at his sleeves, which came down about as far as his thumbnails, then, when he had disengaged his hands, picking his nose while he looked over at Alick's leading hotel, the Bentley, across the street, described by the Louisiana State Guide as "a six-story building of brick and stone, with a columned façade and a richly decorated interior." He stared at it as if it contained some absorbing riddle.

When he had finished with his nose, he began to bathe his face, his temples and the back of his neck with Coca-Cola from the cold bottle, sloshing it on like iced cologne.

"Cool yourself off, Earl," a voice piped up from the crowd, and the Governor shouted back, "I'm a red-hot poppa."

When he had wet himself down sufficiently, he drank the heel-tap and set the bottle down. Then he lit a cigarette and smoked, dramatically, with the butt held between his thumb and middle finger and the other fingers raised, in the manner of a ventriloquist. While he smoked right-handed he pulled out his handkerchief and blotted his wet face with his left.

He sat unheeding of the rumpus raised by his adherents, like a player in a jazz band who has finished his solo, or a flashy halfback who poses on the bench while the defensive team is in. The candidates ranted and bellowed, putting across a few telling although familiar points.

"In the great state of Texas, biggest and richest in the United States, there is an old-age pension of thirty-one dollars a month. Here in Loosiana we got seventy-two."

But the bored crowd stood fast, knowing that a whistle would blow and the star would throw off his blanket and come onto the field again to run rings around the forces of Mammon. Sure enough, after what seemed to me an endless session of subordinate rant, the Governor threw away the last of a chain of cigarettes and shook his head like a man waking up on a park bench and remembering where he is. He got up and walked to the microphone so fast that the man using it had barely time to say "I thank you" before the Governor took it away from him.

"You shall know the truth, and the truth shall set you free," the Governor said, "but you will never get to know the truth by reading the Alexandria *Town Talk*. You all read in that paper that I am crazy. Ohyeah. Do I look any crazier than I ever did? I been accused of saying the fella that owns that paper is a kept man. Maybe he ain't, but I'd like to be kep' as good as he is. He married a rich woman. That's about the best way I know to save yourself about ninety-eight years' hard work."

"Amen, Earl, it's the truth," the old man in front of me

cried, and the Negroes laughed at what was apparently a well-established local joke.

"Maybe some of you are here because you've never seen a man out of a nuthouse before," the Governor said tolerantly. "Maybe you want to see a man who has been stuck thirty-eight times with needles. Oh, the first man stuck me, stuck me right through the britches. He didn't get me in the fat part, either, and oh, how it hurt! Maybe I lost a little weight, but you would have, too. Occasionally I say hell or damn, but if it had happened to you all, you'd say worse than that. Christ on the Cross Himself never suffered worse than poor old Earl!

"Oh, not that I'm fit to walk in Christ's shoes!" he bellowed to preclude any confusion. "I'm not good enough, when a fellow slugs me on one cheek, to turn the other side of my scheming head. I'm going to slug him back."

"Amen, Earl. You tell him, Earl. Who you goin' to hit first, Earl?"

"Down there in that court in Texas in Galveston before that Texas judge, I felt like Christ between the two thieves. He reared back his head and he said, 'Father forgive them, for they know not what they do!'"

At this point he was interrupted by wild handclapping from a group of elderly ladies wearing print dresses, white gloves, straw hats and Spaceman eyeglasses, who had been seated quietly on the platform through the earlier proceedings. They were under the impression that it was an original line.

I next remember the Governor in his seat again, head down, exhausted, having given his all to the electorate, in a pose like Bannister after running the first four-minute mile. It occurred to me that he was like old blind Pete Herman fighting on heart alone, by a trained reflex. Pete is a friend of the Governor's.

As Earl sat there, one of the assisting speakers, a fellow with a strong voice, grabbed the microphone and declaimed the family battle ode, "Invictus."

When the man came to the part where it says:

> "Under the bludgeonings of fate
> Ma haid is bloody, but *unbowed*"

Earl flung up his head like a wild horse and got up like a fighter about to go into a dance to prove he hasn't been hurt. He called for a show of hands by everybody who was going to vote for him, and I waved both of mine.

I left him surrounded by children to whom he was passing out coins, "a quarter to the white kids and a nickel to the niggers."

My companion had rejoined me after parking the car, and we walked together through the breaking crowd.

"How could his wife have done him like she done?" a woman was asking another, and a man was saying, "Got to give da ol' dawg what's coming to him."

My friend saw Gravel, a handsome, tanned man in a white sports shirt and black slacks, standing where the lawn ended at the pavement, and walked over to him. Two or three reporters were already there, asking Gravel what he had said when Earl said what.

The National Committeeman said he had come to hear the speech because two or three men close to Earl had called him up and warned him that Earl was going to blacken his name.

"I wanted to be there to nail the lie," he said. He said Earl started the argument.

Six or eight of the ten Gravel children played hide-and-seek around their father's legs, and as he talked, another boy, about eleven years old, ran up and said to a slightly younger girl, his sister, "The Governor wanted to give me a quarter, but I wouldn't take it."

"Why not?" the girl asked, and I decided she had a bigger political future than her brother.

Gravel said he had to go home because there was a wedding reception there, and the rest of us walked back toward the Bentley, where all the rocking chairs on the porch were already occupied. The row of glowing cigar ends swaying in unison reminded me of the Tiller Girls in a glow-worm number.

CHAPTER VI

THE BIRD THAT KICKS

I thought Uncle Earl had been great, but a couple of press-association men who had been covering him for years said that he looked overtrained. After his first speech of the day at Leesville, the seat of Vernon Parish, they said, he had had to make a detour to his home farm at Winnfield and have a half-hour nap and eat a piece of watermelon before he could continue the day's round.

Then he had gone on to Coushatta, the seat of Red River Parish, and Jena, the chief place of LaSalle Parish, picking up steam as he went along, sitting next to the driver in the front seat of the air-conditioned limousine. He keeps the rear seats free for bodyguards and the things he buys at the wayside as he travels: pitchforks, country hams, post-hole diggers, goats, and cases of Dr. Pepper, 7-Up, Louisiana and out-of-state beers, and sacramental wine. It's his way of getting into conversation with people, and he likes to bargain with them —another Arab trait.

104

"Do you know he came back from Galveston with fifteen pounds of okra that he bought at the nuthouse farm because the price was right?" one reporter asked me. "And we got all the gumbo in the world in Louisiana. Why, Dick Leche told me that one time when he was Governor and Earl was Lieutenant Governor, about 1938, they went to a convention out in Chicago, and the day before they left they stopped by Marshall Field's store to buy some presents.

"Dick says, 'When da salesgoil wrapped up all Oil's poichases—' you know how Dick talks, with that Orleans Parish accent—'Oil says, "How much is it?" and she says, "Twenty-two dollars." Oil says, "Dat's ridiculous, I'll give you sixteen." ' Dick tried to pretend he wasn't with him.

"The girl said salespeople weren't allowed to change prices, and Earl said he wanted to see the manager of the store. The girl went for her boss, and he sent for his, until the head man came, and Dick says Earl didn't get the package for sixteen dollars, but he got it for twenty and a half.

"When they were outside, Earl said, 'Marshall Field or a little store in Winnfield is just the same. Dey'll all take a little less if you hold out.' "

We moved into the Bentley cocktail lounge, a big, air-conditioned basement room, as cheerless as the crypt beneath the Egyptian temple in *Aïda*. The Bentley was built in 1908 by an Alexandrian lumber king who thought Alick was destined to be a metropolis; like a parent buying clothes for a growing boy, he took several sizes too large.

The reporter who had been telling Long stories continued: "Dick likes to say, 'Dey talk about da boid dat fouls its own nest, but Oil is da guy who kicks ovuh his own applecart.' "

"Dick's right," another fellow said. "When Earl is out in front, he gets too rough, and he starts acting out front as soon as he thinks maybe he will be. With all those croakers agreeing he was crazy a while back, a lot of politicians thought he really *was*. So they started cutting him out of the jackpots. Now he wants to punish all of them at once. Naturally they're going to stand together against him. What he should do is play sweet until he gets re-elected, and then go after them later.

"But instead of that he calls a special session for August 11. That's a week from Monday. And he's going after Theo Cangelosi, the chairman of the board of supervisors of L.S.U., the State University, because he says Cangelosi sided with Miz Blanche against him when she put him in the crazy-house. Cangelosi was Earl's own lawyer, and Mrs. Long's too. Earl needs a vote of two thirds of the Legislature to can Cangelosi, and it means a row with everybody who believes in keeping the State University out of politics. Besides that there are a lot of Italian voters. He's kicking over his own applecart."

Olmsted wrote of Louisiana politicians in 1854: "A man who would purchase voters in the North would, at least, be careful not to mention it so publicly," and the difference persists, to the great advantage of conversation in Louisiana. We were joined by a lawyer who said he would like to be district attorney in his parish because that's where the money could be made. The incumbent, who had made plenty, was willing to move up to the bench, for a reasonable monetary consideration, because it was secure and dignified. The lawyers and the D.A. were sure they could swing both interim appointments, and if they did they could dig in solidly by doing favors before next election time.

But the old judge in the district, although infirm and due soon to retire for age, wouldn't quit a day sooner because he did not care to go on half pay. The fellow telling the story, the would-be district attorney, had offered to pay the judge the difference between half pay and full pay for the rest of his term, but the old fellow wanted the whole sum in advance.

"It ain't right," the attorney said, "because he don't figure to live that long, y'unnerstand?"

In a while I went up to bed, and before I turned out the light read the verso of the pink throwaway I had acquired at the meeting. It said:

A Message From
GOVERNOR LONG

This is a special invitation to my friends and all the people of this area to come out, bring your friends and neighbors, and learn the truth about what I have done, and what I have tried to do for you while serving as your Governor.

Ye Shall Know the Truth and the Truth Shall Set You Free

I also want to tell my people who have been so faithful to me just how I have been treated. I want you to personally see me and hear for yourself the harassments I have been subjected to. I want you to know the truth and not be guided by the rumors which have been spread among the people and which have been printed in the Alexandria *Town Talk*. Not all of the newspapers and reporters are bad. Many of the newspaper reporters are my personal friends. Some are ugly, and are inflicting upon their readers a great deal of sordid material that is distasteful. Some, but not all, of these newspapers and photographers, have been hounding me all day and all night like a pack of hounds after a wounded animal, scenting blood, trying to catch him and pull him down. They won't allow me—a sick man—a little privacy in which to recover from being dragged, without my permission, through three hospitals. I know you will agree with me that they have somewhat kept me from looking after our state business, which I have been daily doing even while I am trying to rest. I can tell you, as my office force well knows, that I attended to the affairs of state by giving of my time from 12 to 15 hours a day while I was out of the state. Only when you know the truth can you judge for yourself what the facts are.

Father, Forgive Them; For They Know Not What They Do

I do not propose to punish those who have had me locked behind ten doors, and had to have a key to turn on the lights, I would not hurt any one of them even though they have vilified me and almost wrecked my physical well-being. To those who have helped me in so many ways, I want to personally shake your hand and thank you for your prayers, your letters, and all the help you have given me. Were it not for your prayers, I would still be locked up by so-called friends who forbid my true friends from getting to me.

Wherefore By Their Fruits Ye Shall Know Them

As long as I have lived, I have been a friend of the less fortunate. I have always worked to improve their lot, and am still working to do so. These small-loan lobbyists who bleed the poor must be stopped! It is wrong for them to take advantage of the poor people. And it is wrong to railroad sane persons into insane asylums, where they do not belong, just because somebody wants to get rid of them for their own selfish purpose. After being dragged around, I know now personally how many of our people are mistreated in those hospitals. And I am going to wage a fight against those who thrive, prosper and live like kings on the misery of the mentally sick in this state. I want to help these poor, unfortunate people.

Your Help Is Needed

After being dragged through three different hospitals, locked up and jailed, in less than 30 days and losing 40 pounds, I am pleased to tell you that I have gained back nine pounds and hope to gain more. I continue to solicit your prayers and assistance during the months ahead. If the good people of Louisiana continue to stand by me as you have in the past, we will by the Grace of God win our battles against those who would take advantage of the poor, the mentally sick, and those of our people in less fortunate circumstances.

COME OUT AND HEAR THE TRUTH!

THE TRUTH SHALL SET YOU FREE!

The lobby was still acreep with politicians when I came down to breakfast next morning.

On the way down to the Coffee Shoppe my guide spotted our up-from-the-Third-Ward lawyer friend.

The lawyer was a Comiskey man. And Jim Comiskey had, as of Wednesday evening last, been the most enthusiastic Long booster I had encountered. This was Sunday morning.

"How do you think our boy looked?" I asked jovially, sure that with him at least I knew who "our boy" was.

"Who do you mean, our boy?" he asked. "We're going with Davis."

"When did you go off Earl?" I asked.

"He's got no chance," the Comiskey man said. "Did you hear him last night? Fighting with everybody in the state. Nobody can trust him. The sheriffs can't trust him. He'd send state troopers in anywhere if he didn't get what he wanted. The money people don't trust him either; he'd put a tax on sulphur, tax on timber, tax on gas, if he took the notion. He'll always have the newspapers on his neck. He's crazy.

"Besides, how does he know the Supreme Court will okay this scheme to resign and then come in again? What happens if it doesn't work?" There was fury in the lawyer's fair, handsome face now, the fury of a man taking a runout.

There was political logic in the move of traditionally incompatible factions to Davis. The newspapers and the money people, implacably hostile to Uncle Earl, were not sure of beating him with Morrison, whom they had backed of old. But the Mayor of New Orleans was a good campaigner, and what with the bad publicity Earl had been getting lately and the new enemies Earl delighted in making, Morrison might make it a close race in the first primary.

In the event Morrison did, only he and Earl would run off in the second primary. Then, if Earl blew his top again, or the Supreme Court turned him down, it would be too late for the Old Regulars to get behind a third candidate.

Morrison would win, and that, to the R.D.O. and the gamblers, was the worst thing that could happen. Morrison had taken away the R.D.O.'s municipal patronage. If he went to Baton Rouge he would take the state patronage too, and the R.D.O. would expire.

The forces of respectability that could not tolerate Long, and those of sin, which could not tolerate Morrison, had thus a poolable, swappable negative interest in the primary. The *Picayune* crowd had only to chuck Morrison, and Comiskey to chuck Long.

Uncle Earl had once said of Davis, "He won't say nothing, he won't promise nothing, and if he gets in, he won't do nothing." These are the qualifications of the ideal compromise candidate.

Outside, Alick lay prostrate under the summer climate of Louisiana, like a bull pup flattened by a cow. Night had hidden nothing of its charm—there was nothing to hide. I wondered what a well-kept man did with his time.

"At a place called Alexandria, our progress was arrested by falls in the river which cannot be passed by boats at low stages of the water," Olmsted wrote of Alick when he visited it in 1854. "The village is every bit a Southern one—all the houses being one story in height, and having an open veranda before them, like the English towns in the West Indies. It contains, usually, about 1,000 inhabitants, but this summer had been entirely depopulated by the yellow fever. Of 300 who remained, 120, we were told, died. Most of the runaway citizens had returned when we passed, though the last cases of fever were still in uncertain progress."

It is not much of a place now, but it must have been hell then. I have sometimes thought that the Deep South—Mississippi, Alabama, northern Louisiana and eastern Arkansas—resembles an iceberg floating upside down in the sea of history. The iceberg, dear to after-dinner speakers, shows only a fifth of its volume on the surface.

The Deep South has gone on for a hundred visible years since the Civil War bemoaning the twenty-five years of its own total history that preceded. In this submerged fifth of its past, according to the legend, great "floating palaces" went up the majestic rivers (since sullied forever by Yankees washing their feet in them) to thriving cities (like the Alick of 1854). Short-order aristocrats, rich from cotton made on new land by prime Negroes, built the great houses, and elegance busted out all over.

Joseph G. Baldwin, in 1853, wrote the pleasantest contemporary text on this period: *The Flush Times in Alabama and Mississippi*. Baldwin was an immigrant from Virginia, not a Yankee, and he lit out for the gold fields in California in 1849. *The Flush Times*, in 1853, was reminiscence. Since Baldwin wrote before the War, his work has none of the *de mortuis nihil nisi* piety of the writers during the hundred years above the waterline. He writes of a vulgar, swindling, money-grabbing time, when homicide and practical jokes about equally divided the boomers' leisure moments.

The boom was already over when he wrote. From the beginning of the rush for cotton lands, in the 1830s, to the beginning of the War, in 1861, was a span shorter than separates us from the administrations of Herbert Hoover and Jimmy Walker. This included the Caliban beginnings, the making of the money, the achievement of elegance, and the historic split-second left for the elegance to harden—like a quick cake icing. This knockabout-comedy turn in history has furnished forth the brooding squashy ancestral memories of a hundred Faulknerian heroes, *echt* and *ersatz*.

It is as if, in 2029, the whole nation should blame all inter-

vening misfortunes on the stock-market crash of 1929, and
think of the few years of money-making—for atypical people
—that preceded 1929 as a thousand-year Reich of Stutz Bear-
cats for Everybody. I opened my mind to my friend when we
got on the road again, and he, since he was from New Orleans,
took no offense. In New Orleans a planter was always a figure
of fun, a pigeon to pluck.

"The South doesn't believe the story," he said, "except
when it seems useful to pretend to believe it. That's why I
can't read Faulkner. And one of the bonds between Earl Long
and his audiences is that he doesn't believe it, and they don't
believe it, and it's a kind of private joke between them, like
two kids in Sunday School that don't believe in God."

On the way out of town the old station wagon jogged along
for a while beside the turbid, yellow Red River, celebrated
in hillbilly song. The Governor had retired for a day of rest
to his farm at Winnfield, in Winn Parish, about fifty miles
north of Rapides.

Tom said that the parish voted Populist in the 1890s, when
the poor white-Populist leaders were taking over power in
other Southern states—Pitchfork Ben Tillman in South Carolina, Tom Watson in Georgia, Jeff Davis in Arkansas. But
the downstate "aristocrats," who had their counterparts in
the states named, had a unique advantage in Louisiana in
the alliance of the heavy-voting New Orleans city machine.
The machine ran the wide-open city and the oligarchy ran
the state. So the revolt within the Southern Democratic party
that took place almost everywhere else was delayed in Louisiana until the emergence of Huey Long. That accounted for
part of the added bitterness.

"They sat on the lid an extra thirty years," Tom said.

We ourselves were bound for Baton Rouge, where the Governor was slated to hold a press conference on Tuesday, and where, in the meanwhile, I hoped to find a couple of people I wanted to talk to. We took the route that leads directly to the Mississippi this time and followed its west bank down, instead of taking the overland diagonal between Alick and the west end of Baton Rouge bridge. This was better. There were old towns in a pastoral country like Angoulême, French names on the R.F.D. mailboxes and the general stores, cattle and even sheep under the trees in the fields by the way through Marksville and Mansura.

We stopped in a *guinguette* on the bank of False River, a long, narrow lake that once was an arm of the Mississippi, isolated by a shift in the river's course. The *guinguette* was a dicotyledon; within one plank shanty were two saloons, one for white and one for colored, divided by a partition. They had, of course, separate entrances. The white side was empty of customers when we arrived, the colored full of racket and animation. The old station wagon was the only car at the white entrance; there were two or three Oldsmobiles and an MG at the other.

To my regret we had to drink on the gloomy side. The licensee was white, a Monsieur Lejeune, who pronounced his name Ledjoon. The bottles were on the white side, but Monsieur Ledjoon spent most of his time serving the colored. We felt left out and, after a drink, pushed on, to arrive after dark in Baton Rouge, where on Sunday you can't buy a drink at all.

Baton Rouge is not only the state capital but a boom town.

In 1940 it had a population of 34,000, which has risen since to an estimated 150,000. The population of New Orleans has increased only by twenty per cent in the same period. Oil refineries and chemical plants using the by-products of oil are the main factors in the industrial growth.

The factory chimneys, suggesting the laboratory of a titanic alchemist, are floodlighted at night. The old paddle-wheel steamers converted into ferryboats, crossing and recrossing the vast river, look like hansom cabs on an autobahn, or if you like to put it the other way, the factories look like paintings Niles Spencer slapped down against a Currier and Ives background. I reviewed the confusion of epochs from my bedroom in the Capitol House, a vast hotel on the bluff overlooking the river. It reminded me of the night when on the George Washington Bridge, bound for Manhattan, I encountered a raccoon determinedly padding his way back to the New Jersey shore.

I spent Monday nonpolitically, beginning the day with a drive to St. Francisville, north of Baton Rouge, to see an elegant, gracious old pre-War-Between-the-States mansion named, I think, Rosedown. (All elegant, gracious mansions dating from the Flush Times have names like pre-War-with-Spain blocks of flats on the West Side of Manhattan.) The excursion was the idea of a lady who accompanied us and insisted that not to see at least one great house would leave me with an unbalanced view of the state.

When we reached the gates of the great house, hospitably inscribed "No Visitors," we learned that Rosedown had new Texas owners (for my own sake I was glad they were not Yankees), who were home in Dallas attending the accouchement of an oil field. The caretaker would not let us in. By that time it was raining hard, as it often was in Louisiana that summer, rain that descended in nine-foot cubes with only small airholes between them, so we went back to Baton Rouge.

In the evening I was the guest of a Mr. Lewis Gottlieb, chairman of the board of the City National Bank of Baton Rouge, who gave me dinner at the City Club, the city's social hub. It was a good dinner, built around mallards shot by one of the guests, who emptied his deep freeze in the name of hospitality. There was good wine to drink. But large tears appeared in the lovely violet eyes of my beautiful blond dinner partner, when we had finished the baked Alaska.

"I shivah when I think of what you are going to write about us," she said, "having a man like Earl Long for Govunuh of the State of Loosiana. Oh, please tell the fine people up North that we ahnt all like that! There ah fine, decent people in the State of Loosiana, just as there ah in New York and Chicago."

When I told her that Uncle Earl was, for the moment, my favorite American statesman, she professed not to be able to believe me. I thought of the ghost-written *Time* speeches recited by national figures, and for the moment I believed myself. I could not imagine Robert Montgomery coaching Uncle Earl.

"Would you rather have Kefauver as Governor of Louisiana?" a man across the table asked her.

"Oh, Kefauver," she said doubtfully, "I don't know whether I would."

"Or Fulbright?" said the man, playing it straight.

"Yes, Fulbright," the lady said unexpectedly, "yes, I believe I'd rather have even Fulbright," and she looked very grave. It confirmed my opinion that Uncle Earl was the most effective liberal south of Tennessee.

"How about Warren?" the man asked.

"Warren?" the lady repeated. "What Warren do you mean?"

"The Warren who's Chief Justice of the Supreme Court," the tease specified.

"Oh, *him!* the lady cried, in a voice that indicated a joke could go too far. "I'd much rather have little old Earl Long."

CHAPTER VII

HENRY LUCE'S SHOESTORE

Next day, with Uncle Earl expected to appear at the Man-sion at four in the afternoon, I called on Theo Cangelosi, his *bête noire,* in the morning.

The attorney was a long, bony man, with the long, bony face of a Savonarola, a likeness particularly noticeable in the nose and chin. He practiced law in one half of a double white clapboard house on a wide, shady street near the Governor's mansion.

"People suffering from Earl's affliction frequently turn against their nearest and dearest," he said. "Their anger is in proportion to their affection before they took sick. Earl is under the impression that I helped Mrs. Long get a first mort-gage on their new house for forty thousand dollars and that she kept the money, but I never even saw the cash. I just sent the papers to the bank. Both Earl and Blanche signed them, and if he didn't get his share it's his own fault." Mr. Cangelosi looked sad and injured. "Now Earl's putting out that Blanche shared the money with me," he said.

"Earl really turned against me when I wouldn't help him try to escape from that hospital in Texas, but I just didn't want him to get into trouble. I went down there to see him when he sent for me, and the first thing he said was, 'I'm pretty good at getting around people, and I've been talking to the guards on this floor, and I believe that if I had a thousand dollars in cash I could bribe my way out. You take this note and go back to the City National Bank at Baton Rouge and get me the money, ya hear, and I'll be all right.'"

Mr. Cangelosi took from a desk drawer a slip of ruled yellow paper and showed me the message, in the wobbly script of a man having a lot of trouble. "Treasurer, Louise Gottlieb, Earl Long Campaign Fund Account, City National Bank, Baton Rouge, Please pay over to bearer $1000 in $100 bills. —Earl K. Long"

The Governor was an old friend of Lewis Gottlieb, the bank chairman, but he had spelled Gottlieb's name Louise, indicating considerable residual confusion at that moment. (The 38 shots had not, perhaps, worn off.)

"I heard that somebody did slip him fifteen hundred dollars," I said.

"Yes," said Mr. Cangelosi, "but that was later, at the hearing, and it wasn't me. I was trying to protect him. If one of those guards had taken his money and then shot him trying to escape, I would have blamed myself forever. I have always acted in his best interests."

I thanked Mr. Cangelosi and walked out into the blood heat and down to the bank to confirm the existence of an Earl Long Campaign Fund.

Mr. Gottlieb, looking little like a Louise, said there was such an account, but it wouldn't be ethical to tell me how much there was in it. I surmised that there might suddenly get to be a lot in it if the Income Tax people ever disputed the Governor's blanket contention that the money people hand him is intended as campaign contributions. He might then formalize the status of cash in hand by making a large deposit.

"I imagine Earl is up in Winnfield making catfish bait for the special session," Mr. Gottlieb said. "He's probably putting together a program of legislation aimed to give every senator and representative something for himself: a bill to appropriate funds to widen a road in one parish, a bill to raise the salary for a kind of job some senator's cousin has in another. That's the kind of thing Earl's good at—knowing every local politician in the state and remembering where he itches. Then Earl knows where to scratch him."

Lunch in the Capitol House confirmed my theory of culture belts. The Capitol House lies within ninety miles of Galatoire's and Arnaud's in New Orleans, but its fare bears a closer resemblance to Springfield, Illinois, where a distinguished hostess once served me a green salad peppered with marshmallow balls. So Dover, within twenty-three miles of the French coast, eats as un-Frenchly as the farthest side of England.

A statewide convention of high-school football coaches was in session, and there seemed to be hundreds of them—a cross between the plantation overseer and Y.M.C.A. secretary. In the night they congregated over bottles of bourbon, building character for transfusion to their charges in the fall, and in the day they attended seminars on whipless slave-driving and how to induce adolescents to play on two broken legs.

The Governor's Mansion at Baton Rouge, like the State House, is a monument to the administration of Huey Long. The story goes that the Martyr, when he gave the architect his riding orders, said he wanted a replica of the White House so he would know where the light switches were in the bathrooms when he got to be President. Huey lived in it from 1930 to 1932, and Earl inhabited it briefly for the first time in 1939, when he filled out the term of the unfortunate Mr. Leche. After that he lived in it again as Governor from 1948 to 1952 and began a third tenancy in 1956. When I saw it, Longs had been masters of the house for ten out of the nineteen years of its existence, almost enough to give it status as an elegant old gracious family mansion. Earl and Miz Blanche had built their new house in a newer and more stylish part of Baton Rouge, before the Governor decided against moving.

Tom and I arrived half an hour before the hour appointed for the Governor's press conference. We were in company with Margaret Dixon, editor of the Baton Rouge *Morning Advocate,* one of the few people in Louisiana who could usually get along with Earl. Mrs. Dixon, handsome, stable and strong, has a firm, serene personality. She is the kind of woman motherless drunks turn to instinctively to tell their troubles with their wives.

"Earl is the funniest man in the world," she said over her shoulder as she drove. "Life in the Capitol would be dull without him. Did you hear what he said to Leander Perez, the States' Rights man, the other day? 'What are you going to do now, Leander? Da Feds have got da atom bomb.' And when Blanche went to live in the new house, he said she had 'dis-domiciled' him. He has a style of his own—he's a poet. He said he was so groggy when he got off the plane that took him to Houston that he felt 'like a muley bull coming out of a dipping vat.' I don't know why it should, but the 'muley' makes that line sound a hundred times funnier. It just means without horns."

"It particularizes the image," I suggested. "Bull is a word so general that it blurs: the dumb bulls in Spain, the tight bulls in fly-time. 'Muley' makes you see a bull of a peculiarly ineffectual kind."

"You sound more like Huey," Mrs. Dixon said. "Earl says, 'Huey tried that highbrow route and he couldn't carry his home parish. I carry Winn Parish every time.'

"He praises Huey up, but he never misses a chance to mention when he does something better—in 1956, when he won the Governorship on the first primary, without a runoff, the first thing he said was 'Huey never done that.' "

Now we were on the Mansion driveway lined with laurel and packed with press cars.

Inside, the press had taken over, as if the Mansion were the scene of a first-class murder and the cops were still up-stairs. Reporters in large groups are ill at ease, and they try to make up for it by acting too easy. Each is preoccupied with his own time situation—his paper's deadlines and the accessi-bility of telephones. Each, before a public conference, shapes in his mind what would make a good story if the principal said it, and how he can trap him into saying it. If the principal delays his appearance, the reporter begins to wonder whether he will have time to write the story. Then, with further delay, he begins to wonder if he will have time to telephone. Next, he gets angry. He resents his subjection to the whims of his inferiors, and he vents his resentment by a show of elaborate contempt.

We turned left inside the fanlighted door and went down a couple of steps into a great reception room furnished like a suite in a four-star general's house on an Army post, where the furniture comes out of quartermaster's stores. The bleakness of such pieces, all bought on contract sale, increases in proportion to the square of their sum: two hotel sofas are four times as depressing as one; three, nine times. The Governor's drawing room, of good height and proportions, contained at least twenty-six paired pieces, all covered with pink or green brocade chosen for its wearing qualities. The mauve drapes were of the tint and gloss of the kind of spun-sugar candy that is usually filled with rancid peanut paste; the carpets were a flushed beige. There were two wall mirrors reflecting each other, a blackamoor candelabra, three chandeliers, and no pictures. There was not a piece of furniture from before 1930 nor a portrait of a former Governor or his lady. I wondered where the loot from the old Mansion was.

Huey had cleared out the lot, as a link with the hated aristocratic past. As it was, it made a perfect waiting room—a place in which boredom began in the first ten seconds.

At half-past four the Governor's press secretary, an intimidated former state senator named Fredericks, appeared at the top of the two steps. He announced that the Governor's party had telephoned from the road: they were still about fifty miles from town, and the Governor had given orders to serve cake and coffee to the reporters and tell them to wait. Negro servants in white jackets served coffee and sponge cake, both good. A couple of the bloods of the press who covered the beat regularly had found their way to some bourbon concealed from the rest of us and came smirking back.

One fellow went about canvassing colleagues to join him in a walkout. He proposed that everybody go off and leave the Governor flat—insult to the press, showing up so late. That would let him see where he stood. His colleagues, knowing where they stood, paid no heed.

An hour passed, and the Governor's party arrived. State troopers shoved us back, and the Governor's party headed straight upstairs, to "wash up and be right back." A minute later, word came down that the Governor was going to shave. The Negroes served more coffee, this time without cake. Nobody talked of leaving now.

A reporter with good connections learned the cause of the long delay from a state cop who had ridden in the convoy. "Governor stopped at a few farms along the way to buy some guinea hens, but he couldn't get the right price on them."

Forty-five minutes more, and the Governor made his entrance. He hadn't shaved but had taken a nap and put in a telephone call to a woman friend in Alick. Fortunately for the press, she had not been at home. Once on the line, he talked for hours.

Mrs. Dixon said that this was his first press conference in the Mansion since deputy sheriffs, whom he called bone-crushers, had hustled him down his own steps and into an ambulance on the night of May 30.

He was wearing a black mohair suit even less elegantly adjusted than the one at Alick, and a sober necktie of black with atom-bomb mushrooms of white and magenta. He moved to a seat in the middle of a long sofa with its back to the cold fireplace. There, crossing one leg over the other knee, which exposed his white cotton socks, he faced his familiar persecutors with the air of a country Odysseus home from a rough trip, with no Penelope to greet him.

This Odysseus didn't care if he never set eyes on Penelope again. A woman reporter asked him if he was going to make it up with Mrs. Long, and if he didn't think that would help him get the women's vote in the primary.

He said, "If dat's da price of victory, I'd rather go ahead and be defeated. After all, lots of men have lost elections before."

Somebody asked him if he was set on the special session of the Legislature and he said he was, that the call would go out before five o'clock the next day. That was the latest moment when he could call a session for Monday, August 11. The Governor must include with the call a list of the legislation he means to propose; none other can be voted at the session. He said he was readying his list.

A reporter asked him if he would include any new tax bill, and he said no, if the state won its suit against two oil companies, "we might get by with no taxes at all." But if the money did not come in that way, he would try for some new taxes at the regular session. This was a flat assumption that he would run and be re-elected.

He had already said that, rather than cut state services, he would be in favor of "any kind of a tax but a sales tax, because that falls on the poor devil."

Now he began again to lay into the rich people, who "wanted to cut out the spastic school," but the reporters, who had heard that number in his repertory, managed to get him off on Cangelosi.

"There never has been a man who *mis*used and unduly *ab*used my confidence like Cangelosi," the Governor said. "If he hadn't a done me like he done, and rubbed it in, I might forgive him, but that long-legged sapsucker made more money than any man I ever knew," he said, adding quickly, "of which I have not participated in any of the profits."

The Governor's moist hazel eyes, filled with sweetness, clouded over at the memory of what he had suffered. His voice, low and hoarse at the beginning of the conference, as it well might be after the weekend of stump-speaking, rose indignantly, like a fighter knocked down by a fluke punch.

"They misled me," he said. "The reason I was feeling so poorly at the last Legislature was I had kept on postponing an operation that I was to have at the Oshner Clinic in New Orleans. When my sweet little wife and my dear little nephew got me to go on that plane, they told me a damn lie that I was going to Oshner for my operation.

"Then when they got me to the plane the bonecrushers strapped me to the stretcher and a doctor stuck me through the britches with a needle. My wife and my nephew promised they would come right down to Oshner next day to see me. But the plane flew me to Gal*ves*ton, and my sweet little wife hasn't showed up yet, neither my little nephew. When the plane landed me at that airport, there, they told me I was going to a rest house, where I was promised a double bed and quiet. The doctors gave me pills to make me sleep. First I took them one by one, then by the papercupful. Then I got to chunkin' them in there by the wad. While I was in that condition, they got me to sign a thing that I wouldn't sue them for kidnaping. I went contrary to what my lawyers would have wanted." This, I learned long later, was precisely true. His Texas counsel believed he had his transporters cold under the Lindbergh Act.

Uncle Earl looked out at the reporters with bottomless pity in his eyes, as if he were recounting the ills, not of one storm-tossed traveler, but of all our common kind.

"They snatched me out without even enough clothes on me to cover up a red bug," he said, "and a week after I arrived in Texas I was enjoying the same wardrobe. They put me in a room with the door open and crazy people walking in and out all night; one of them thought it was the toilet."

"Pardon me," said a lady of the press, interrupting, "but what was the operation you were expecting?"

"I guess you can guess," the Governor answered, and he pointed down. "On my lower parts."

He was still intent on his sorrows. "Then, this Corner here," he said. "Wasn't he a nice judge to commit me to Mandeville when I come back? We been on opposite sides in politics as long as I remember, but if the position had been reversed, I might have given him a break. And Bankston, the superintendent, a man I appointed myself, could have left me out, but he wouldn't. But I got out, all right. I put *him* out and *got* out."

"Governor," a reporter queried, "what is your personal opinion of who's going to win this election?"

"I am," the seated orator replied without hesitation. "Uncle Earl. It's going to be a case of Katy bar the door. Little old Dellasoups Morrison will be second."

"And third?" pursued the questioner.

"Jimmie Davis, if he stays in the race," the man who picked himself said. "And little Willie Rainach and Big Bad Bill Dodd a dogfall for fourth." In country wrestling, a dogfall means that the men lose their footing simultaneously and both go down, which makes that fall a draw.

"We going to have a party here tomorrow, a homecoming party for the press," he said, "and you are all invited. Going to have something for everybody—religious music over here on one side of the room and honky-tonk on the other. But no Bedbug Blues—that's Jimmie Davis' tune."

There was a good deal of the discourse that I have not recorded. Carried away by the stream of idiom like a drunk on a subway train, I missed a lot of stations.

Somebody asked the Governor what he thought of the Luce publications' having asked for a change of venue to a Federal court in his libel suit for six million dollars. He said he didn't care what kind of court the case came up in.

"They going to find themselves lighter and wiser when it's over," he said. "The Luce people been going on too long picking on people too poor to sue them, and now they're going to get it in the neck. Mr. Luce is like a man that owns a shoestore and buys all the shoes to fit himself. Then he expects other people to buy them."

This was the best thing said about publishers, I felt, since I myself wrote thirteen years ago: "To the foundation of a school for publishers, without which no school of journalism can have meaning."

I put all my admiration in my glance and edged my chair up to the end of the Governor's sofa. When I try, I can exude sincerity as far as a lama can spit, and the Governor's gaze, swinging about the room, stopped when it lit on me. My eyes clamped it in an iron grip of approval.

I inched forwarder, trying not to startle him into putting a cop on me, and said, "Governor, I am not a newspaperman. I am with you all the way about publishers. Nor am I primarily interested in politics. I came all the way down here to find out your system for beating the horses."

An expression of modest disclaimer dropped like a curtain in front of the cocky old face.

"I got no particular system," he said. "I think I'm doing good to break even. I think horse-betting should be dissected —into them that can afford it and them that can't. I think if you can afford it it's a good thing to take your mind off your troubles and keep you out in the air."

"Do you play speed ratings?" I asked. The Governor, in his eagerness to talk simultaneously about all phases of handicapping, choked up—it was the bronchiectasis—and began to cough.

Quickly, I offered him a lemon drop and he accepted it. Once it was in his mouth, I knew, from my experience among the Arabs in the opposite end of the interrupted sea, that I had won. He had accepted my salt, now he would reciprocate. The bronchiectasis struggled with the lemon drop for a moment and then yielded.

The Governor's throat cleared, and he said: "Yo'all stay'n' eat."

"Y'all stay, too," the Governor said to Miss Dixon and Tom and a couple of the other press people. "There's aplenty." I imagined he must have a great surplus of supermarket

bargains in the larder. "Just set here and wait. We got a lot
to talk about."

The reporters and television men who had deadlines were
already clearing out. Earl shouted after them, "Y'all come
back and I'll say this—" But they, who had waited for him so
long, had had enough.

CHAPTER **VIII**

BLAM-BLAM-BLAM

There had been so many people in the room, and for so long, that they had taken the snap out of the air-conditioning. The men staying on for dinner—about fifteen of us—took off their coats and laid them down on chairs and sofas.

One of the women guests, a Northerner, inadvertently sat on a jacket a political gent had laid aside. It was a silvery Dacron-Acrilan-nylon-airpox miracle weave nubbled in Danish-blue asterisks. She made one whoop and rose vertically, like a helicopter. She had sat on his gun, an article of apparel that in Louisiana is considered as essential as a zipper. Eyebrows rose about as rapidly as she did, and by the time she came down she decided that comment would be considered an affectation.

A colored man brought a glass wrapped in a napkin to the Governor—"Something for my throat," the latter explained— and the members of his inner council gathered at his flanks and knees for the powwow on catfish bait. One of the bills

Earl had in mind would give individual members of the
Legislature scholarship funds to allot personally to young
people in their districts. Another would raise the salaries of
assistant attorney generals, whose friends in the Legislature
might be expected to respond. There were various local baits,
funds for construction. The compounders kept their voices
low and mysterious, as if saying "One-ha.. pint of fish oil, one
ounce of tincture of asafetida, one ounce of oil of rhodium—
that will fetch them," or "Mix equal parts of soft Limburger
cheese and wallpaper cleaner—never fails." Sometimes a con-
spirator would be unable to suppress a laugh.

A Mr. Siegelin, a political catfisherman arriving late,
brought with him two children, a girl of about ten and a
boy of five.

"Give them Cokes," the Governor said, and while a state
cop hurried off to fill the order, he said to the little girl,
"I hope you ain't going steady yet."

The little girl shook her head, and Uncle Earl said, "That's
right. I went with more than a hundred before I made up
my mind."

Made it up too soon at that, he probably thought, as he
wondered about Miz Blanche and the mortgage money.

The children took their Cokes and settled down on facing
identical love seats to drink them, while their father, a fair
man in shirt sleeves, sat down to join in the bait suggestions,
with his equivalent of "Cut smoked herring into bits. Soak
in condensed milk several days." The group was still in the
midst of bait-mixing when a plug-ugly, either a state trooper
or a bodyguard from civilian life, came to the top of the steps

leading to the dining room and shouted, "It's ready!" By his tone I judged him ravenously hungry.

The catfishermen remained engrossed in their concoctive deliberations, and the plug-ugly shouted at Mrs. Dixon, whom he judged less engaged, "C'mawn, *Maggie!*"

Mrs. Dixon rose, and the catfishermen, Southern gentlemen after all, perforce rose too and rushed toward the dining room in her wake, the Governor dragging the two children.

The ballroom smacked of Bachelors' Hall, lacking the touch of a woman's fastidious hand, but the dining end of the Mansion, I was happy to see, was well kept up. The long table under the great chandelier was covered with a mountain range of napkins folded into dunce caps, with streams of table silver in the valleys between them, and the iced tea, Sargassified with mint and topped with cherry, was pretty near *Ladies Home Journal* color-ad perfection. Negro waiters and waitresses swarmed about, smiling to welcome Odysseus home. None of them, either, seemed to miss Penelope. The wanderer, his heart expanding in this happy atmosphere, propelled me to a seat at the head of the table.

He took his place at my left, with the Northern lady across the table from him. Around the long board crouched plug-uglies in sports shirts, alternating with the guests: Tom, Mrs. Dixon, Senator Fredericks, Siegelin, the two Siegelin children clutching Coca-Cola bottles, and half a dozen politicians I hadn't met. The colossal figure of Mr. Joe Arthur Sims, the Governor's personal counsel, dominated the other end of the table. Mr. Sims had his right arm in a plaster cast that kept his hand above his head, as if perpetually voting Aye. He had sustained an odd sort of fracture on July 4, he explained.

It had followed hard on his stump speech for the Governor, a great oratorical effort, but he denied that he had thrown the arm out of joint. He said he was in an auto crash.

The Governor said, "We don't serve hard liquor here. Da church people wouldn't like it. But I'll get you some beer. Bob," he called to one of the somber seneschals, "get da man some beer." Quickly, the waiter fetched a can, two holes newly punched in the top, ready for drinking, and set it down on the table.

The beer bore an unfamiliar label, and the Governor said, "Dat looks like some of dat ten-cent beer from Schwegmann's." (He had probably bought it himself, on one of his raids for bargains.) "Dat looks like some of da stuff dat when da brewers got an overstock, dey sell it to da supermarkets. Get da man some *good* beer. And bring a glass—hear?"

He looked so healthy now that I ventured a compliment.

"You fooled those doctors, all right," I said. "You're like that Swede Johansson—you have your own way of training."

"You see dat fight?" the Governor asked, suspending his attack on the salad, which he was tossing between his dentures with the steady motion of a hay-forker. I said I had.

"I didn't see it, but I would have if I thought da fellow had a chance to lick Patterson," the Governor said. "Patterson's pretty good." (If he looked at the return fight, he was let down again.)

"I hear they've got a law here in Louisiana that a white boy can't even box on the same card with colored boys," I said.

"Yeah," said the Governor, "but dat kind of stuff is foolish. If dere's enough money in it, dey're bound to get together."

I recognized the theory of an economic resolution of the race conflict.

He sat there like a feudal lord, and his *maisnie,* the men of his household, leaned toward him like Indians around a fire. The trenchers went around, great platters of country ham and fried steak, in the hands of the black serving men, and sable damsels toted the grits and gravy. There was no court musician, possibly because he would have reminded the Earl of Jimmie Davis, but there was a court jester, and now the master called for a jape.

"Laura, Laura," he called out to one of the waitresses, "set your tray down—dere, hand it to Bob. Tell us what your husband does for a living."

"Prize fighter, sir," the girl said.

"Show us how he does when he goes in da ring," the Governor ordered.

The girl, long, thin and whippy, was instantly a-grin. This was evidently a standard turn, and she loved the spotlight. She got rid of the tray and showed how her husband climbed through the ropes, lifting her right knee high to get over the imaginary strand, and holding the hem of her short skirt against the knee as a boxer sometimes holds his robe to keep it from getting in his way. Once inside, she danced about the ring, waving her clasped hands at friends in the imaginary crowd. Then she retired to a corner and crouched on an imaginary stool until the Governor hit the rim of a glass with a gravy spoon.

The girl came out, sparring fast, dancing around the ring and mugging for friends at ringside, with an occasional wink. The opposition didn't amount to much, I could see. Laura's husband, impersonated by Laura, was jabbing him silly. Then her expression changed; the other man was beginning to hit her husband where he didn't like it. Her head waggled. She began to stagger. Even the bodyguards, who must have seen the act often, were howling.

"Show us how your husband does when he gets tagged," the Governor ordered, and Laura fell forward, her arms hanging over the invisible ropes, her head outside the ring, her eyes bulged and senseless.

The feudal faces were red with mirth. I applauded as hard as I could. Laura stood up and curtsied.

"You gonna let him keep on fightin'?" the Governor asked.

"I don't want him to," Laura said, "don't want him get hurt. But I don't know if he'll quit."

"Is he easier to live with when he loses?" a state senator asked.

"Yes, sir, he is," the jester said, and took her tray back from the colleague who had been holding it.

The meal went on.

"Dat's da way some a dese stump-wormers going to be when dis primary is over," Uncle Earl said. "Hanging on da ropes. If it's a pretty day for the primary, I'll win it all. I'll denude dem all, da *Times-Picayune* included."

Outside the air-conditioned keep the enemy might howl, but inside, the old vavasor held his court without worrying.

"Da voting machines won't hold me up," he said. "If I have da raight commissioners, I can make dem machines play 'Home Sweet Home.'" He laughed confidingly. "Da goody-goodies brought in dose machines to put a crimp in da Longs," he said. "Da first time dey was used, in 1956, I won on da first primary. Not even my brother Huey ever did dat.

"Da machines is less important dan who's allowed to vote," he said. "I appointed a man State Custodian of Voting Machines here dat run up a bill of a hundred and sixty-three thousand dollars for airplane hire in one year, just flying around da state, inspecting da machines. Good man, Southern gentleman—da *Times-Picayune* recommended him and I thought I'd satisfy dem for once. Den he got an appropriation from da Legislature to keep da machines in repair, but it said in da contract with da voting-machine company dat da company had to keep dem in repair for one year for free. So he split da money wit da company—dey sent him six thousand dollars, and den another six thousand, but I grabbed half of da second six thousand for my campaign fund. Should have took it all."

The cellarer he had sent for the name-brand beer returned with a report that none except the supermarket kind was cold.

"Dey keeping da good beer for demself," the Governor said indulgently. "You drink dis." It tasted fine.

The Northern woman, who had listened with awe to the career of the voting-machine man, asked, "What happened to him?"

"I denuded him," the Governor said. "It's an electoral office now."

"And where is he now?" the woman asked, expecting, perhaps, to hear that he was confined in a *cachot* beneath the Mansion.

"He's hypnotizing people and telling fortunes and locating

oil wells," the Governor said, "and he got himself a fine blonde and built her a big house and quit home."

Outside of the *Lives of the Troubadours,* which was compiled in the thirteenth century, I had never known a better-compressed biography. I felt that I knew the denuded hypnotist well. I remembered the comparable beauty of the Governor's account of the last day of a beloved uncle in Winnfield: "He got drunk and pulled a man out of bed and got into bed with the man's wife, and the man got mad and shot my poor uncle, and he died."

I asked him what he thought of Governor Faubus of north-neighboring Arkansas, who had won a third term by closing the schools, and he said Faubus was a fine man, but nobody had told him about the Civil War.

"Fellas like Faubus and Rainach and Leander Perez and da rest of da White Citizens and Southern Gentlemen in dis state want to go back behind Lincoln," he said. "And between us, gentlemen, as we sit here among ourselves," he said, arresting a chunk of fried steak in mid-air and leaning forward to give his statement more impetus, "we got to admit dat Lincoln was a fine man and dat he was right."

Then, as he turned back to the steak, skewering it against a piece of ham before swallowing both, he caught my look of astonishment and cried, too late, "But don't quote me on dat!"

Since he has won his last primary, I disregard his instructions. It was a brave thing for a Governor of Louisiana to say and would have made a lethal headline in his enemies' hands: "Long Endorses Lincoln; Hints War Between States Ended."

We had up another can of beer, and the Governor and I shared it with a sense of double complicity.

"Laura, Laura," the Governor called to his jester, "get rid of dat tray."

"Yes, sir, Mister Governor," and the star turn passed the grits to a co-worker.

"Now, Laura," the Governor said, "can you make a speech like Mr. McLemore?" (McLemore had been the White Citizens' candidate in '56.)

This was plainly another well-used bit of repertory. The Prize Fighter and Mr. McLemore may be Laura's *Cavalleria* and *Pagliacci,* always done as a double bill. But I'd love to hear her sing Jimmie Davis.

She took a stance, feet wide apart and body stick-straight, looking as foolish as she could.

"Ladies and gentlemen," she said, "do not vote for Mr. Earl Long, because he has permitted da Supreme Court of da United States to make a decision by which, by which, Little White Johnny will have to attend da same school with Little Black Mary. If you wish to prevent dis, vote for, vote for—" and she hesitated, like a man fumbling in his mind for his own name. Then, running her hands over her body, she located, after some trouble, a white card in her breast pocket. The card, a planted prop, showed she had expected to perform. She took the card, peered at it, turned it around and finally read, "McLemore. Dat's it. Vote for McLemore."

The Earl howled, and so did all his guests and men-at-arms. I do not imagine that Penelope would have found it all that funny. She probably cramped his style.

The meal ended with a great volume of ice cream. The

Governor, in high humor and perhaps still thinking of the frustrated voting machines, said to the lady across from him, "Would you mind if I told you a semi-bad story?"

She said she would not mind, and the Governor began: "There was an important man once who had a portable mechanical-brain thinking machine that he carried everywhere with him. Da machine was about as big as a small model of one of dose fruit machines dey have in a Elks clubhouse. When he wanted a answer: How many square feet in a room by so and so much? or, Has dat blonde a husband and is he home? he submitted his question and da machine answered it correctly. He would write out da question on a piece of paper and put it in a slot, da machine would read it, and pretty soon it would go blam, blam, blam—blam, blam, blam—dat was da brain working, and it would give him a printed slip with da correct answer. Well, finally da man got jealous of dis machine, it was such a Jim-cracker, and he thought he take it down a little for its own good.

"So he wrote out a message: 'Where is my dear father at this minute, and what is he doing?' He put it in da slot, and da machine says, 'Blam, blam, blam,' very calm, like he had asked it something easy, and it write out da answer, 'Your dear father is in a pool hall in Philadelphia, *Penn*sylvania, at dis moment, shooting a game of one hundred points against a man named Phil Brown. Your dear father is setting down watching, and Phil Brown has da cue stick and is about to break.'"

"Philadelphia, *Penn*sylvania," had the romantic sound in the Governor's mouth of Coromandel in Sinbad's.

The Governor's manner changed, and his voice became

indignant. " 'Why,' da man says, 'dat's da most unmitigated libelous slander I ever heard of. My dear father is sleeping in da Baptist cemetery on da side of da hill in *Pitts*burgh, Pennsylvania, and has been for da last five years. I am sure of da dates because my dear Mother who is still living reminded me of da anniversary of his death and I telegraphed ten dollars worth of flowers to place on his grave. I demand a *re*-investigation and an *apology*.'

"And he writes it out and puts it in da slot. 'Dis time I got you,' he says. 'You ain't nothing but a machine anyway.'

"Da machine reads da message and gets all excited. It says, 'Blam, *Blam*' and 'Blam, *blam*,' like it was scratching its head, and den 'Blam, blam, blam, blam . . . blam, blam, blam, blam,' like it was running its thoughts through again, and den 'BLAM!' like it was mad, and out comes da message."

All eyes were on the Governor now, as if the ladies and men-at-arms half expected him to materialize the ticker tape.

"Da message said, 'REPEAT,' " the Governor said. "It said 'REPEAT' and den, 'RE-REPEAT. Your dear father is in a pool hall at Philadelphia, *Penn*sylvania, playing a game with a man named Phil Brown. YOUR MOTHER'S LEGALLY WEDDED HUSBAND is in the Baptist cemetery on the side of the hill in *Pitts*burgh, *Penn*sylvania, and has been there these last five years, you BASTARD. The only change in the situation is that Phil Brown has run fourteen and missed, and your old man now has the cue stick. I predict he will win by a few points.' "

It broke everybody up, and soon the Governor said to the outsiders politely, "Y'all go home. We got a lot to do tonight." But he said he might be able to see me at nine next morning.

I arose at that hour and got over there, but there were already so many cars on the driveway that if it hadn't been morning I would have guessed there was a cockfight in the basement. Inside the Mansion, the nearly bookless library on the right of the door that serves as a waiting room was full of politicians, all wearing nubbly suits and buckskin shoes, and each sporting the regulation enlargement of the left breast beneath the handkerchief pocket. (This group included no left-handed pistol shot.) The length of the queue demonstrated that the public reaction to the speeches had been favorable, and that the sheiks who had raided the herds in Earl's absence were there to restore the stolen camels.

A Negro in a white jacket came in and asked the ritual "Y'all have coffee?" Since I had no deal to offer, I just had coffee and went.

Odysseus ruled in Ithaca again.

CHAPTER **IX**

THE BATTLE FROM AFAR

Watching the British general election in the fall of 1959 was, for me, like being at a very dull football game where the only resource is to watch another game on television. Luckily I received frequent batches of newspaper clippings, prefaced by wise notes, that friend Tom sent me from New Orleans, where the good game was.

The change from Louisiana was depressing; it was like trying to taste Empire hock after a dozen Sazerac cocktails.

Instead of calling each other "common damn hoodlum" or "little pissant" in the Louisiana fashion, the British candidates discussed interminably whether the country could afford an increase of $1.40 a week on the old-age Pension. The Tories, boasting the unparalleled pecuniosity of the nation, paradoxically doubted that the economy could stand the strain of the dollar forty. An option of Gaitskell or Macmillan thrilled like the choice between blancmange and Sultana roll on the menu of a British railway hotel. But there I was. I had booked my seat in advance for the wrong game.

British elections were not always so dull. William Cobett recalls for us a great moment when he stood for Coventry in 1820, at the age of 57:

"Just at this moment one of the savages exclaimed, 'Damn him, I'll rip him up!' He was running his hand into his breeches pocket, apparently to take out his knife, but I drew up my right leg, armed with a new and sharp gallashe over my boot, and dealt the ripping savage so delightful a blow, just between his two eyes, that he fell back upon his followers."

It was the kind of do that Earl Long would have appreciated. Once, years ago, in the vigor of political discussion, Earl bit a man. Later he preferred a diet of grits and fried steak. When I left, Earl looked like winning a fourth term if he had luck. I kept looking back over my shoulder until I reached the exit.

The first collection of clippings from Tom showed that Earl had run into trouble. This was normal. The fine Governor fought best when he was on the bottom. His scheme to win renomination in the Democratic primaries, resign as Governor the day before election and then be elected looked sure to succeed. The State Supreme Court, which would have to rule on the constitutionality of the maneuver, appeared firmly in his favor. His martyrdom in Texas had won him the sympathy of the rural voters.

"Wouldn't you rather have a tried and true man, half crazy and half intelligent, than some bladderskite?" he asked one cheering crowd.

One of my last political memories before I left the Great

State was of the Governor devising political catfish bait. The cat is not a fish to be taken on bird feathers with whimsical names. It demands the solid attraction of chicken guts surrounded by an aura of asafetida: "Smells bad, but cats love it," the manual says.

But other hands had been setting other trotlines with baits even more persuasive to the legislators, I learned from Tom's first note. The statesmen showed up as in law bound at Baton Rouge on August 11 to answer the Governor's call, but once there and in session they voted instantly to adjourn. They left the baits on his hooks untouched; they did not seem to be hungry.

Even in the face of such wholesale defection Earl had maintained tradition, I was glad to note from the enclosed clippings. His Lieutenant Governor had said to him, "Now, Earl, don't get upset," and the fine Governor had answered, "I am upset-proof." This was in the Spirit of "Invictus."

Earl was still the betting choice, Tom wrote, but he no longer had an organization he could rely upon. When some of Earl's hand-fed legislators turned on him, he felt like a British colonel in the Sepoy rebellion. But, after all, British rule in India survived the uprising by ninety years. Tom wrote that with the field for the nomination still wide open Earl was the favorite at 4 to 1, with other serious possibilities at prices ranging from 13 to 2 upward.

The relative showing of the candidates who finish third, fourth, fifth, and on down the line in the first primary, and so are eliminated, has its own significance. It serves to establish the price each expects to be paid for his support in the second run.

The rerun system gives them a chance to salvage part of their losses. In a close race between the two top men, a candidate who finishes a good third can often turn a handsome profit. Even a man who finishes down the list can sometimes make a good thing of it if his votes include a particularly deliverable bloc—say a group of parishes where his family bank owns a mortgage on every farm. It is all delightfully Middle Eastern.

I read Tom's letter and the accompanying clippings from the *Times-Picayune,* over tea in the Central Hotel in Glasgow, where I was fortifying myself for a great Tory mass meeting in a moving-picture cathedral—admission by ticket only. Mr. Macmillan, aggrieved and sniffling, would read his voters a lecture on how they had never been so well off and how chaps who wanted to spend the dollar forty had better look out where they were going to get it. I was glad, for the sake of the people around me, that there were no runoff elections in Great Britain. Two such campaigns in one year would be beyond bearing.

Nostalgic, I read a quotation from Uncle Earl: "Jimmie Davis loves money like a hog loves slop."

The next tidings I had from New Orleans were more serious for the fine Governor of the Great State. The Democratic State Committee had declined to receive his candidacy unless he resigned as Governor before September 15, the day on which entry fees were due. This was not law, but house rules, and the Committee made up its rules as it went along. Earl had farsightedly pre-ascertained the attitude of the Supreme Court, but he had failed to win the State Committee first. The ultimatum left him with a hard choice.

If he resigned at once, in order to run, he would forfeit seven months of power and patronage, from September 15, 1959, to April 18, 1960, the day before the vestigial election. During that time, the Lieutenant Governor would be Governor, free to fire all Earl's appointees and put in his own, and to make all the deals that Earl would otherwise have the opportunity to make. More, an ex-Governor is in a less advantageous position to campaign than a Governor. Worse, the Federal people, all Republicans, were known to be hot on Earl's trail with a mess of Income Tax charges.

"I'm the most investigated man in history," he said.

Earl was sure that in an age when States' Rights are again fighting words, the Feds would not seek an indictment against a Governor in office. Out of office was another matter.

These were heavy immediate advantages to risk on a chance of winning what looked like a hard campaign for renomination (and would be harder when he lost control of the state payroll). A *Times-Picayune* report of an attempt to interview him showed that Earl was preoccupied. The reporter called the Governor's hotel room and asked to speak to him.

A voice, Earl's, answered, "He's just gone up in a balloon."

Tom's next letter apprised me of the hero's decision. "Our boy apparently got what he wanted and can now pull down," the letter said.

Tom is the last independent source of news left in New Orleans. He is in the situation of the RAF hero who was 30,000 feet in the air, without an aircraft.

A couple of accompanying clippings carried denials by Internal Revenue officials and by United States Senator Allen Ellender, Senior Senator from Louisiana, that Ellender had talked to Federal officials and squared the Internal Revenue rap against Long. Denials, in Louisiana, are accepted as affirmations, and it is held a breach of the code for a public man to deny anything that isn't so. Ellender is an old protégé of Huey Long's. The Senator is therefore the last man in the world to suspect of denying anything you couldn't bet your bottom dollar on.

Tom continued, "The Old Regulars have bolted to Davis." There was a whiff of magnolia about the item. It is *de rigueur* that the first leader to declare himself for a candidate should also be the first to cut his throat.

Jimmie Davis, to whom Comiskey had bolted, was, I knew, a singer and composer of hillbilly music ("You Are My Sunshine," "Nobody's Sweetheart Now") who had been Governor of Louisiana from 1944 to 1948 but had spent a good part of his term in Hollywood making a movie about a hillbilly singer who got to be Governor.

Tom now turned to deLesseps S. Morrison who, when I left, seemed Earl's most formidable rival for the nomination. "Chep, the progressive conservative, had chosen quietism and decency in making his play for the rational crowd here," Tom wrote. "He went back to Pointe Coupee, his home parish, to announce for Governor last weekend. Then he got on water skis and sprayed up and down False River, speaking to the crowds at the boat piers. Chep is making the Chamber of Commerce approach: no gimmicks, only a circus bandwagon and a jazz band, which he is using on his stumping tour through the towns. But Davis has a good thing going in Old Rugged Cross. Looks like he's going to whip Chep by a parasang, but you never know about Louisiana."

The "Old Rugged Cross" referred to Davis' campaign tech-
nique of visiting men's church clubs with a choir of professional hillbilly singers who harmonized on hymns. They
accompanied the hymns on guitars.

When I read this letter I was in a "small hotel in a good
neighborhood" in London, struggling with the vertebrae of
a kipper, which refused to come loose from the flesh.

I tried to imagine the Prime Minister stumping Clydeside
from the Clyde on water skis or Mr. Gaitskell playing a guitar
to the electors, but I failed.

I tried to imagine the kippers were soft-shell crabs just
bursting out of the old carapace, full of fat stored against the
ordeal of fasting while the new shell hardens. Busters, they
call such crabs in New Orleans. I failed again. I was in the
wrong country, politically and gastronomically.

Clippings of a later date accompanying the letter said the
fine Governor had decided not to run to not immediately
succeed himself.

The next batch cheered me. Tom's covering letter was
dated September 19, and as it had been mailed to New York
and then forwarded, it reached me late in the month. The
British campaign was well bogged by that time. Since neither
party produced any news, the newspapers had taken to head-
lining the public-opinion polls. The polls found an ever increasing number of people who said they didn't know how
they were going to vote. The headline writers christened these
the "Don't Knows." Headlines on a day, as the struggle approached its climax, were: "Don't Knows Swinging to the
Tories," or "Don't Knows Lean to Labor," or just "Don't Be
a Don't Know."

In Louisiana, Earl had induced an old political enemy named Jimmy Noe to form a ticket with him: Noe for Governor, Long for Lieutenant Governor. In the days of Huey, Noe had been a red-hot young politician, but he had subsequently devoted himself to oil wells and radio stations and had not run for office since 1940. He was rich. But Long would supply most of the strength for the ticket. Tom said anti-Long people feared that if Noe were elected Governor he would resign immediately in favor of Long.

Tom also sent along the official entry list. There were eleven candidates for Governor, and as many for each of the state offices. Of the gubernatorial candidates five were likely to poll a sizable state-wide vote. The others were small investors, hoping to scrabble together enough votes to trade in for small state jobs if they endorsed the right man in the runoff primary. One, Tom wrote me, was a specialist in soliciting subscriptions to his campaign. He had a sucker list of country people to whom he would promise high office after his election if they would just send him a couple of bucks. This pro sometimes made as much as five thousand dollars running for Governor.

The serious candidates besides Davis, Morrison and Noe were Willie Rainach, the professional segregationist, and the schismatic Longite whom Earl called Big Bad Bill Dodd. There are false Imams as well as Imams among the Longites. All Longites agree, though, on a program of soaking the oil companies and raising up the humble. Noe and Dodd, therefore, would hurt each other.

There was no great political profit in race hatred in Louisiana, because Morrison and Long, for years the chief rivals for the crown, both favored Negro voting rights and a "reasonable" race attitude. The White Supremacy people had no place to take their votes. They had to let them be guided by other issues or else stay home on Election Day.

Earl used to contain the Rainach threat by equating him with the NAACP in "trouble-making." ("I suspect Rainach and the NAACP are just playing 'You goose me and I'll goose you,' " my hero once said.)

As to Dodd, Tom wrote, "Bill Dodd's campaign isn't getting anywhere, so he has made a deal to throw to Morrison in the runoff."

He added, "I keep thinking of that Morrison going Jesus-like on water skis to the assembled throngs on the shores of the Galilee of Pointe Coupee Parish. 'I will teach ye to be fishers of men and not fishers of fish.' Election night ought to be a good show here. It always is. Will you be back in the U.S.A.?"

The date set for the first primary was December 5, 1959. I was back in the U.S.A. a couple of days after Thanksgiving. I emplaned at La Guardia on the afternoon of Thursday, December 3, and was at Moisant Airport, New Orleans, a few hours later.

The banishment of Aristides because his townsmen were tired of hearing him called "the Just" was one of the triumphs of the Mediterranean mind. It constituted public recognition that a crook is more easily tolerated than a man who makes his virtue a damned nuisance.

When I got to New Orleans, it appeared that the electorate had slated Chep Morrison for the Aristides treatment. In the plane on the way south I read a great bale of clippings that had been waiting for me in New York. The star item was a front-page editorial from the *Times-Picayune* of Sunday morning, November 15, under the heading

ELECTION OF DAVIS AND AYCOCK RECOMMENDED

For fourteen years the paper had been plugging Morrison, the debonair reformer. His white plume was the highest feather in its hat. He had accepted the Reform nomination for Mayor on three days' notice in 1946 and had won.

Morrison has suppressed open public gambling in New Orleans—the horse rooms are now across the river in Jefferson Parish—and at least has forced lamp shades on the red lights. Concurrently he has permitted the strip-tease joints to flourish. He has thus aided in the substitution of vicarious lechery for the real thing, keeping New Orleans in step with the nation. It is my guess that he has kept the town tighter than his political rivals will admit; this guess is based on the hostility he inspires among cab drivers and bellboys.

In addition to these negative activities, in which the *Times-Picayune* took editorial satisfaction, he has transformed the city. These building feats have given Morrison the fame, rare in the South and usually repugnant to its voters, of a man who gets things done. These facial transformations are the only extant monument to the paper's political effectiveness. In state politics, the *Times-Picayune* has been to the Longs what the Austrian armies were to Napoleon. It made their reputation by being easy to lick.

His social graces endear him to news weeklies—he neither drawls nor gets his elbows in potlicker, and he can shake a hand as briskly as Richard Nixon. Each time Morrison has been candidate for Mayor, the *Times-Picayune* has supported him and claimed credit for his victory over the Organization, which usually appeared in its cartoons as a hog with a high hat wallowing in a trough labeled "Corruption." In 1956 it had backed him for Governor against Earl Long plus the Organization, and he had been resoundingly beaten.

Now the *Picayune* was dropping its perennial candidate and joining the hog in the high hat behind Jimmie Davis. The editorial said:

"This newspaper urges Louisiana voters to support Jimmie H. Davis and C. C. Taddy Aycock in the December 5 election. . . .

"Our recommendation of Mr. Davis is no disparagement of the achievements of Mr. Morrison. We simply do not believe that Mr. Morrison would be in a position to rally various political factions and consolidate diverse legislative elements in support of a forward-looking and effective program for the whole state. . . .

"In making our choice of Mr. Davis over Mr. Morrison, we undoubtedly will be accused by some of playing politics. . . .

"Many knowledgeable experts feel that Mr. Davis will surely win and that Mr. Morrison, even if he should reach a second primary, will lose to any of the major candidates who may oppose him. This may be true and may serve as a basis for some for preferring Mr. Davis.

"But it is not our basis."

Clipped to the editorial was a report of a stump speech by Willie Rainach, the States' Rights man, at a metropolis called Napoleonville. Rainach quoted a *Times-Picayune* editorial in 1947, when Davis was in office, that said, "When the going gets hot, the Governor disappears."

The "little pinheaded nut," as Earl called Rainach, had picked up one recruit of stature, in fact of the most stature of almost anybody I know—"Little Eva" Talbot, once a legendary football lineman at Tulane, the leading New Orleans university. "Rainach called attention to the fact that New Orleans attorney and oil operator W. H. Talbot had joined his campaign as a member of the advisory committee," the clipping said.

"In a statement from New Orleans, Talbot said he was disappointed in Davis, and therefore had joined Rainach."

A vast, gusty man, Little Eva is a landmark in downtown New Orleans as he makes his way from his air-cooled office to his air-cooled automobile and back, waving a hand the size of a football at admirers. He is one local athletic hero whose shadow has never grown less. He has made a lot of money.

The *Times-Picayune* quoted Talbot as saying, "Senator Willie Rainach is the only man in the race who will help us fight the States' Rights battle.

"States' Rights includes segregation but it includes a lot of other things too, such as making the Federal Government keep its nose out of the gas and oil business in Louisiana."

It was a powerful and succinct statement of what lies behind much in the South that otherwise seems irrational.

Big Bad Bill Dodd, who had already pledged his support to Morrison in the runoff, was denouncing Morrison in a town called Rayne. Dodd said, "The nothing Davis rendered and the nothing of Chep's promises are a poor substitute for Dodd's proved record and practical progressive platform."

As for Rainach, Dodd compared him with John Brown and Hitler.

Tom's brief note of interpretation said: "Davis is running a nothing campaign, but I guess maybe the early form chart making him the favorite was right. Morrison is running a better campaign. But Davis seems to have access to those mysterious submerged factors of power in La. You figure it out. The conniving between first primary and runoff ought to be fantastic."

For added entertainment on the way down I had a couple of handouts from Rainach headquarters. One, a mimeographed sheet, said:

WORKERS FOR RAINACH

No other candidate in this present contest can begin to match the record of Willie Rainach in fighting off the attempt of the Federal Government to control every phase of our existence. The record of DeLesseps S. Morrison is by far the worst, inasmuch as he has consistently refused to even protest the racial integration ordered by Federal despots in Washington. It is common knowledge that the New Orleans Police Department has planned to cooperate with any Federally ordered integration of New Orleans Schools. No man in the Police Department relishes this plan, but the Police, under Morrison, will be powerless to stop him. The United States District Court has ordered this integration in New Orleans schools to be carried out in March—NO LESS THAN SIX MONTHS FROM THIS DATE.

With Willie Rainach as Governor of Louisiana, Morrison and his NAACP and negro Longshoremen henchmen will have no chance to control the City of New Orleans. With

Morrison as Governor, all of Louisiana will quickly find itself in the midst of strife such as that presently being experienced in New York City, Detroit, Chicago and other cities where politicians permitted the NAACP to have its way. THE FIRST CHILD MURDERED IN AN "INCIDENT" MAY BE YOUR OWN!

Jimmie Davis sings and says nothing. Davis is content to be known as a "sweetness and light" candidate and refuses to "be critical of my opponents." This is the proper attitude for a glass-house dweller.

DO NOT BE TAKEN IN BY THE PROPAGANDA THAT "RAINACH IS A GOOD MAN BUT HE HASN'T A CHANCE," OR BY THE COMMUNIST COINED CLICHE THAT "SEGREGATION IS NOT AN ISSUE." Ask the parents of the murder and rape victims of the Eastern cities what happened when segregation ceased to be an issue. The white people in these areas are now fighting for their very existence.

The other was a printed pink throwaway that read:

REPRINT OF LETTER TO JIMMY DAVIS FROM F. A. WALLIS
Zachary, Louisiana, Oct. 12, 1959

Dear Jimmy:

I voted for you when you ran for Governor before. I like you personally, and have been inclined to vote for you again. However, I have been doing a lot of soul-searching on this Governor's race. I have reluctantly come to the conclusion that I cannot vote for you this time. I think I owe it to you to tell you why:

The next Governor of Louisiana is going to be under tremendous pressure to integrate our public schools. The South is slowly but surely winning the battle for public opinion in the minds of the white people of the North. But if we are to win, we must stand firm and unyielding during the next administration. We don't want our children to be the guinea pigs in sociological experiments. The rapes, murders and violence that have followed integration of the schools in New York, Chicago, Philadelphia, Washington and other Northern cities must not happen to our children. And if we are to win, we must have a Governor *who will not yield*. Jimmy, you are a professional entertainer. We all know that the NAACP has the entertainment field by the throat. Why, you—as a professional entertainer—if you were Governor of Louisiana, would be at the mercy of the NAACP! The NAACP forced the entertainment world to rewrite the great songs of Stephen Foster! Will this crowd be easier on you than they were on Stephen Foster?—

If you as Governor of Louisiana dared to fight the NAACP, not a record of yours would be sung over television, radio or in a juke box over this Nation. You would be blacklisted from the night clubs and entertainment halls of this country. If you as Governor of Louisiana should dare to lead a fight on the NAACP, you would be through as a professional entertainer, and you know it—and I know it!

I shall vote for Willie Rainach, who has led the fight for segregation in this state, who has shown that he has the courage and ability to lead us to victory—a man who is not vulnerable to NAACP attack!

Sincerely your friend

/s/ F. A. Wallis
Zachary, Louisiana

Neither emission said anything about the oil department of the States' Rights question.

They served to distract my attention from the dismal airplane dinner dumped down before the passengers at five-thirty in the afternoon, as if we were patients in a military hospital. The steak was of some plastic material like Silly Putty, and only as warm as the small glass of domestic champagne that accompanied it. At current air speeds, the dinners aboard are redundant, but they are kept on, I suppose, because they are a part of the fixed rate the companies are allowed to charge for transportation. This is as if railroads were allowed to include in the price of a ticket from New York to Springfield, Massachusetts, a handsome charge for a bad meal whether you wanted it or not.

CHAPTER **X**

OYSTERS AND LARCENY

The taxi driver who took me in from the airport to my hotel did not think a Catholic could win. (Morrison is a Catholic.) So he would stay on as Mayor until 1962, when he will have to retire.

"What do you think will happen to him?" I asked.

"Oh, he's well fixed," the driver said. "Got all that money hidden down in Argentina."

A New Orleans taxi driver whose favorite candidate was accused of honesty would feel hurt. It would mean that you thought the driver capable of backing a damned fool.

My hotel, the St. Charles, had been since the previous summer officially styled the Sheraton-Charles, but is never so referred to. The first two versions of the St. Charles burned; the present was built in 1891. I was glad to see the hotel chain had changed nothing but the name, and that, as I have mentioned, ineffectually. It is a bit as if they bought Grant's Tomb and then named it the Sheraton-Grant's Tomb. The

hotel was still a warren of austere rooms above a colonnaded
lobby of Sistine magnificence—an architectural allegory of
the Old South.

Tom was in the lobby when I got there. There was just
time to catch the end of the great Davis windup rally at Jeru-
salem Temple of the Mystic Shrine, he said.

The meeting was just breaking when we got there. Davis is
a Shreveport man, and Shreveport is a dilution of Texas, even
to big hats.

His New Orleans partisans, contrastingly, were members
of the Old Regular Democratic Organization, historically
known as the Choctaws, and the Old Regulars, male and
female, are Hellenistics to the core. They are home-bred
descendants of the famine Irish who came in '47, their assimi-
lates, the German Catholics who came in '48, and their political feudatories, the Sicilians, who came much later. They
intermarry. Morrison, with his Crescent City Democratic
Organization, has cut them off from municipal patronage.
Their leaders consequently live by alliances with the bar-
barian princes from the north, like the Athenian faction
that supported Philip of Macedon.

They run fatter, redder and jollier than either upstate or
French Louisianians. The crowd streaming from the Temple
could have been coming out of a Jim Curley meeting in
Boston or a gathering of Paddy Baulerites in the Forty-third
Ward of Chicago. From the temple, we quickly learned, a
good part of them were going over to a television studio,
where the gubernatorial candidate and his supporting cast
were to re-enact the meeting for rediffusion.

We went along and entered as part of the crowd of enthusiastic partisans. As we went in we were handed "Davis and Aycock" signs on 18-inch cardboard squares. We were to be part of the spontaneous demonstration the television audience would see. The studio was a kind of bus barn. We milled about among the undertakers' chairs provided for enthusiasts until the candidate and his music took their places on a platform facing us. Then we sat down. Then we rose and waved the signs.

I did not recognize Davis, although I had seen hundreds of newspaper and poster portraits of him. This, I discovered when he arose, is because all the pictures were taken head on, with the candidate smiling, and about twenty years ago. Newspaper photographs of Earl Long were usually taken without warning when he was scratching his pants, or when a reporter acting as the photographer's picador had provoked him into a scream of rage.

Davis, I saw, was a sandy-gray man of medium size with a profile like a box tortoise.

He sang a few verses of his campaign song:

> Live and let live,
> Don't break my heart—
> Don't leave me here to cry.

His male chorus, all wearing big hats, helped him out on the refrain. (When he was Governor before, he had most of his band on the state payroll.) Davis then said he had run a clean campaign without trying to hurt anybody's feelings.

John Gremillion, the incumbent Attorney General, who had joined the rush to Davis, next spoke briefly, saying that he had run his own office in "a manner characterized with aggressive efficiency." (Earl Long once said, "If you want to lose anything real good, just put it in Jack Gremillion's law book.")

We all jumped up on signal and waved our signs some more, and a few spontaneous enthusiasts began shouting, "Sunshine!"

The candidate, in response to this demand, rose again and sang all the verses of his greatest hit:

> You are my sunshine,
> My only sunshine,
> I really need you, when clouds are gray . . .

Then the television time ran out.

By that time I was hungry again, and we drove downtown to Felix's, an oyster bar that stays open all night, where you can sometimes hear betting talk.

Sam Sais, the proprietor—I don't know why it is called Felix's—said the primary was so open that he could not quote a betting line. The question nobody could answer was how and in what proportion the four upstate candidates, Davis, Rainach, Noe and Dodd, would split up the Protestant vote.

In New Orleans they eat oysters all year around, but in fairness to the oysters they shouldn't—they are much better in winter. The Louisiana oyster in winter is still a solace to the man of moderate means, sold across the counter, opened, at sixty to seventy-five cents a dozen, and therefore usually eaten a couple of dozen at a time. (I prefer three dozen to any other number of dozen before a meal.) They are wilder and freer than the oysters of Maryland and Long Island and frequently come two or three in a cluster, with rough shells like the little oysters in Trinidad. The oysters share the passionate nature of the human inhabitants of the littoral. They stimulate themselves into what in the less aphrodisiac waters of Gardiners Bay or Chincoteague Island would be considered a population explosion. This accounts for their reasonable price.

The patrons mix their own dope from a variety of condiments oysters do not have to contend with in the North—hot-pepper sauce and olive oil as well as catsup, horse-radish and straight Tabasco. Mixing oyster dope is done as solemnly as the Japanese tea rite.

Tom suggested to me that we go down to Curley Gagliano's place from Felix's because it was the campaign headquarters of a candidate for Governor I had not yet encountered, a statesman named Allen Lacombe, number seven on the ballot.

Gagliano owns the gymnasium where fighters train, on Poydras Street, and an adjoining athenaeum called The Neutral Corner (Poydras and St. Charles Avenue), where good conversation is to be had. Loungers are allowed to buy drinks if they wish, but they are never urged to. Some of the leading philosophers bring their own wine, or Sweet Lucy, and are allowed heat, seat and the privileges of the men's room simply in exchange for their thoughts.

White and colored boxers are allowed to train in the same gymnasium, although a Louisiana state law forbids them to spar with each other. They may not, however, drink in the same saloon. Curley therefore runs a second athenaeum, called Curley's Other Corner, a couple of blocks away. It is for colored.

Curley is a barrel of a man, an old lightweight who never got anywhere and is now unregenerately fat. Men like him are more sentimental about the game than ex-champions, who are often bitter about managers who stole their money. The never-was is less neurotic than the has-been.

Curley is a prosperous bookmaker in Jefferson Parish, across the Mississippi, where he has protection. The gymnasium and the two Corners are his foundations for the arts and he runs them like an endowed retreat.

Curley wears a hat indoors and out. "They call him Curley because he ain't got a stitch of hair on his head," one of the guest philosophers told me.

Curley is a gregarious man but silent, preferring audition to discourse, and is considered a famously easy touch. He maintains solvency only by spending long hours in moving-picture theaters, where he sleeps. "By that way nobody can find him," the philosopher said.

Curley was present, though, when Tom and I entered. So was his candidate, Lacombe, a young-looking man of forty, whose jet-black hair and brows and lashes pointed up a mild, sleepy face, round and pink-and-white. Lacombe, Tom had told me on the way over, was a hustler about town, at times a one-show boxing promoter and at others a handy man around the race-track publicity department. The candidate wore a wide-brimmed, high-crowned oyster-white hat, a string tie, a black worsted jacket and striped pants, the stock cartoon getup for a Southern statesman. His expression was faintly worried, his voice, when he acknowledged Tom's introduction, sweet and almost plaintive.

"Allen is known as the Black Cat," Tom said.

"Bad luck, you know," the candidate explained. "I am the only newspaper handicapper in Louisiana who ever picked seven straight winners at the Fair Grounds and came home broke. I was working for the *Item* then. I got touted off my own selections," he said. He smiled generously, like a small boy showing a festered thumb.

"But I got lucky on the draw for places on the voting machine. I got Number Seven, right between Davis and Morrison. I have to get at least three thousand votes by mistake. I figure to run a good sixth."

He handed me his election card: "Vote for Number 7, Allen G. Lacombe, for Governor," above a picture of his open, honest face and candid eyes, and below it "Vote for Earl Long, candidate for Lieutenant Governor on my ticket."

"Earl gave me the hat," he said, "but he won't come across with nothing. I'm going to get a lot of votes. You'd be surprised how many fellows I talk to that promise me their votes. I take a guy's name and the precinct he votes in, and then I say, 'If I don't get one vote in that precinct, I'll know you're a lying sonofabitch.' "

We sat down at a table with the candidate and Curley and four to six others, and Curley sent to the bar for Cokes or beer, according to tastes.

At that point, a drunk sleeping at a table in a corner of the room woke out of a nightmare and screamed. Disgruntled philosophers, waking off other tables, began to shout, "Throw him out, Goddamighty, can't a man sleep no more?" The man ridden by the nightmare continued to scream, and Curley said, "Take him to the door, Governor." Lacombe got up, and a small, curly-haired man named Blaise said, "Better get that other one over there while you're up, Governor. He wet himself half an hour ago."

Blaise is a journeyman butcher in the French Quarter, I learned later, but he is a volunteer manager.

Lacombe walked over to the screaming man and took him by the hand. He took the other drunk by the hand, too, and led them both gently to the Poydras Street door. He opened the door for them, and they went out without protest.

A moment later they came in through the St. Charles Avenue door. By that time Allen was back at the table with us. Curley laughed. "Cleared their heads," he said. "No harm in them. Toledo Slim, the one who yelled, is a great panhandler when he's sober."

The candidate said, "Like all the other candidates tell, I had a humble beginning, but unlike the other candidates I'm still humble. That's part of a speech I made in Echo, where I was born. That's one town I'm sure to carry. All the voters there are my relatives. It's up near Marksville.

"I hitch-hiked up to Echo a couple of weeks ago, and you'd have thought I was Nelson Rockefeller."

He tried to show that he was not serious, but in the weeks of mock campaigning, his role had grown on him. He was going to miss it when the primary was over. Meanwhile, he was a public figure.

I asked him how it happened that he was embarked on this masquerade, and he said, "Well, I don't have much to do, so I figured I might as well run for Governor. I told Curley I needed two hundred and fifty dollars to post for an entry fee, so he staked me. Afterward he found out I only needed two hundred and ten dollars, and he tried to get the forty back, but I told him I had to have a campaign fund.

"That's the only contribution I've had except for a speech I made to the Pari-mutuel Employees' Union, out at the Fair Grounds. They passed the hat and collected seven dollars and forty-one cents. I got the Volkswagen filled with gas and bet two dollars on the double and blew it. The Volkswagen belongs to the press department at Jefferson Downs that they let me use, but only inside Orleans and Jefferson parishes. So when I go out of town, I hitch-hike."

A customer came over from the bar and said, "I'm going to vote for you, Governor; you're better than them other sons-abitches, anyway."

"What precinct you vote in?" the candidate asked and, after the man told him, said, "Well I'm going to look at the returns Sunday, and if I don't have one vote in that precinct I'll know you're a lying sonofabitch."

The man went away laughing, and the candidate said, "I might even beat Rainach and finish fifth."

"Who do you think will win it?" Tom asked.

"Chep Morrison," the candidate said, "and old Earl will top the list for Lieutenant Governor."

Little Blaise bounced right up on his feet with rage. "Don't tell me Morrison," he said. "You can't walk down the street without somebody mug you and stick a knife in your back. Why? Because all Mr. Morrison's cops are looking for gamblers to shake down. It's easy to catch a gambler. All you got to do, suppose you a cop, is watch da newsstand. A man buy a racing form, all you got to do is follow him. He's going to a bookmaker, ain't he? That's a gambler.

"If I had my way, I'd make a law—a cop catch one gambler, he won't be allow to bring in another *until he arrest a burglar*. You follow me? The cops would catch every burglar in town so they could have a chance to shake down another gambler.

"So how is the element going to vote for Morrison?" He pronounced "element" with accent on the last syllable: "ele*ment*."

"The ele*ment*, you know what I mean, has got all the money in the state. They running wide open in every parish except Orleans. You think they going to back Morrison? He can't beat the ele*ment*. My predicament is—Davis."

An elderly man, lean, worn and wise, joined in: "I hope you're right. The cops own this town. You can't give them an argument. They make a charge without anything to substantiate or coopberate it, and they pull you just the same. If they see a fella in the street and they don't like his looks, they incarcinate him for lerchering and d.a.s.—that's dangerous and suspicious behavior."

A heavy-shouldered old fellow who had been standing up against the bar now pulled himself away and came toward us. When he got away from the bar, he still leaned forward. Tom addressed him politely as "Ice Cream."

The old pushcart man said, "Mister Tom, I went up to the Jimmie Davis meeting, way up in th' balcony, and Jack Gremillion made one of the most powerful speeches you ever heard. Goddamaighty, it was a great oration. But I heard the old men saying, all around me: 'When Davis was Governor before, he cut the old-age pension to twelve-fifty a month.'

And I thought, 'Goddamaighty have mercy on the poor people.' I'm going to vote for Jimmy Noe."

"Jimmie Noe ain't got a chance to be elected dogcatcher," the old cop hater said. Dogcatcher is apparently the hardest office to be elected to in Louisiana. As the campaign wore on, I heard it said of every candidate in the race by his opponents that he couldn't be elected dogcatcher.

"Goddamaighty have mercy on the poor people," Ice Cream repeated.

The argument could have got nowhere, but another gray-bristled ancient entered, and the volatile Blaise went off on a nonpolitical line.

"Balloons," he said, "I heard you had your foot on a twenty-dollar bill and didn't have guts enough to pick it up."

"How could I pick it up?" the old man grumbled, embarrassed. "The fellow that dropped it was looking at me."

"So they tell me you asked the fellow in back of you to pick it up, and you'd split," Blaise said. "And he pretended it was a ten and only gave you five."

"Don't you believe it," Balloons said. "It was a sawbuck, I seen it, and he give me a fin as soon as we got outside."

Blaise said, "Balloons only works once a year, at Mardi Gras. Curley stakes him and he sells balloons. He lives the rest of the year on the profits."

The old man began a chant in Hebrew, and then, breaking off, he said to Blaise, "That's a prayer for the dead, and I'm saying it over you, you should croak."

Blaise, magnanimous, said, "Never mind, Balloons, I'm going to show you what to do when a drunk drops a bill, so you'll know the next time."

He stood up again, looked down, saw the hypothetical bill, no, two bills—Blaise had an inflationary imagination. He stamped his feet down: One, two! covering both imaginary treasures.

"All right, you got them," he said. "One under each foot. Now, watch." He reached into his hip pocket, drew out an extra large handkerchief, spread it for action and then, as he raised it to his nose, dropped it. The handkerchief fluttered toward the floor and Blaise, bending, followed it down as it covered his toes. He reached under the handkerchief and brought it up again, with the putative bills inside. "That way, Balloons," he said, "you don't have to split with nobody."

It was like a program of technical aid to backward countries.

CHAPTER **XI**

DELLASOUPS TOPS THE LIST

It was between three and four in the morning that I returned to the Sheraton-Charles, and I fell asleep to dream of Mr. Macmillan in a big hat and string tie, lecturing the Royal College of Pari-mutuel Clerks on the evils of gambling. Curley Gagliano and Blaise were in the back benches, rising to shout, "Hear! Hear!"

Waking not long before noon, I called the Governor's Mansion at Baton Rouge and, as I rather expected, failed to get through to Uncle Earl. Tom had told me he was at feud with the press and was seeing nobody. But he would be in New Orleans in the evening for a joint live broadcast with his running mate, Jimmy Noe.

There was so much money behind Davis, and Morrison was waging so strong a campaign, with the support of his New Orleans personal organization, that they figured to run one-two. Nevertheless, Earl was expected to eclipse the nonentities running for Lieutenant Governor. I talked on the

telephone with Cousin Horace, the ex-reformer who is re-
nowned for cold, cashable political judgment. He said he had
made a good bet that Earl, running for Lieutenant Governor,
would get more votes than Chep Morrison would have on the
gubernatorial line. And Bob Maestri, a former Mayor, whom
I met later in the day, said in his batrachian voice: "Earl
will be headada list."

This is the kind of romanticism that sometimes fuddles
hardened veterans, like the marshals who threw in their lot
with Napoleon after he returned from Elba. It is the effect
produced by what Max Lerner would call a charismatic personality.

The romanticism did not affect Earl himself; he knew by
then he was on a long shot. It is impossible to organize an
effectual campaign around the prospect of electing a lieutenant governor, because a lieutenant governor has no means
of paying off. He has no power to initiate legislation or veto
bills. He has no patronage to distribute. Thus he can neither
do favors for big backers nor get bread-and-butter jobs for
the indispensable small workers. For a candidate to use his
own money in an election would be as eccentric as a play-
wright risking money on his own play.

I went down to the coffee shop for a late breakfast and
encountered Governor Noe in the lobby. Noe was Lieutenant
Governor in 1936; he briefly succeeded Governor O. K. Allen,
who demised in office. Naturally, he has been called "Governor" ever since.

Noe is a big-headed, short-legged man, protuberating pros-
perously in the middle; his appearance recalls the Herbert
Hoover of Prosperity-is-just-around-the-corner days. Those

were also the great days of "Share Our Wealth" and "Every Man a King" in Louisiana, when Huey was putting on a show as Governor that made the sit-tighters in Washington look even duller than they were.

If Hoover by some disastrous miracle had been re-elected in 1932, Huey might within two years have crystalized around himself all the discontent, rational and irrational, in the country. Roosevelt and his New Deal intervened.

By 1935, when Dr. Carl A. Weiss shot him, Huey was in slashing opposition, and there is a myth in Louisiana that wealthy Republicans supplied him with a secret campaign fund of a million dollars to be used for a flanking attack on Roosevelt in 1936.

The attack would have been a national radical Share Our Wealth party, based in the South, that would take away electoral votes in Louisiana and Arkansas and cut heavily into the left of the Democratic popular vote everywhere. The money was never found, which to the politically conditioned mind of the Great State is proof that it must have existed. Old partisans of Huey's have been watching each other suspiciously ever since.

Noe owns radio stations in Monroe, his home town, and New Orleans, besides the number of oil wells normal in his social group. His New Orleans station has a broadcasting studio in the hotel. He said he didn't know when Governor Long would be coming to town. When I asked him how they were going to run, he was affable but without conviction.

"I think we'll surprise a lot of folks," he said. "They thought old Harry Truman was beat in 1948, but he surprised them."

Truman is the patron saint of short-enders; favorites never invoke him.

Over the coffee, I read the morning paper. There is only one, the *Times-Picayune*. The *States-Item,* same ownership, is alone in the evening. The *Times-Picayune* was full of candidates' advertisements. It is a bitter pill for a candidate to have to advertise in a paper that has been beating him over the head, but there is no other way, until the voters get to the polls, of telling them where, on the scrambled face of the voting machine, to find the names of the candidates forming one "ticket."

Since the election is a primary, there are no symbols or party lines on the machines, nor are the allied candidates aligned vertically. So each advertisement carries the injunction "Tear Out and Take to Polls."

The Noe-Long state-wide candidates on the machine were, for example, numbers 9, 18, 21, 22, 30, 31, 38, 44, 47, and 58, while the Morrisonites had 8, 14, 20, 25, 30 (they endorsed the same man for State Treasurer), 23, 40, 43, and 55.

Only about one voter in two is methodical enough to bring the ad along or not to mislay it. Right at the polls is where the well-organized (tantamount to well-heeled) ticket must have plenty of watchers, plainly labeled as rallying points for the well-disposed, so that they may advise voters.

To rub salt in the wounds of the candidates opposed to Davis, the *Times-Picayune* gave the best spot in the paper, the middle of page one, to a free two-column box headed "This Newspaper Endorses: Governor, Jimmie H. Davis, No. 4," and then the names and numbers of all his running mates down to Custodian of Voting Machines, James Fontenot,

No. 57. At the foot of this box was the addendum "See Sec. 4, Page 8, for other endorsements by the *Times-Picayune* in Orleans, Jefferson, St. Bernard and Plaquemines parishes." These were for candidates for the Legislature and for parish offices, from sheriff down.

It is one of the consolations of a town with one paper, and a dull one, at that, that you have plenty of time to read it. But it is about the only consolation that increasing millions of Americans have, as in more and more cities monopolists buy out the competition.

The owner who sells has the superior consolation of an inflated price, based not on the earning power of his property but on the multiplied earning power of the monopoly after swallowing it. And of this price, if he has owned the property more than a year, the lenity of the capital-gains law allows him to keep seventy-five per cent. If he retains his paper and earns even a moderate profit, graduated income tax will leave him a much smaller proportion. So he has every inducement to sell. This is a fiscal policy aimed at encouraging competitive enterprise by making it more profitable not to compete.

Taking my time about it, I gazed through the advertisements. "The GO Team is the NOE Team," I read; "Elect Noe & Long and Entire Ticket"; "Keep NOE-how in Louisiana's Government a LONG time." There was a portrait of the two candidates, apple-faced and white-shirted, wearing jackets and ties for their city audience, Earl's right arm amicably around Jimmy's back.

The ad got full mileage out of the old Huey Long brags: Charity Hospital Programs, Free School Books (a landmark

in Louisiana education when Huey brought them in) and
Better Roads and Bridges.

Number two paragraph, "Peaceful Race Relations," was
illustrated with a vignette of two clasped hands. Both were
white. The text said:

> This state has had less racial trouble than any other state
> in the South under the Long administration. Yet, the Noe
> and Long ticket stands 100% for segregation and the con-
> tinuance of every southern principle and custom. But it will
> not foster or incite racial or religious unrest.

The first boast was veracious.

The saddest line was at the end: "Paid for by James A.
Noe."

Morrison was photogenic, dynamic, and particularized less:

> LOUISIANA NEEDS Chep Morrison: The only Man with Proven
> Leadership, Experience, Ability to serve *all* Louisiana—Chep
> and His Ticket will Work for You—More New Industry,
> Higher Salaries for Teachers, Maintain Segregation, Better
> Roads & Highways, Increased Old Age Pension, No Increase
> in Taxes, Better Care for Needy and Sick.

And, of course, the names and numbers of the running mates.

Davis had two photographs, both full face and smiling. He
was genially affirmative: he favored Good Government, Long-
Range Planning, Citizen Participation in Government, State
Cooperation in Rodeos, Civil Service, Honest Elections,
Public Access to All Records Except Those Exempt by Law,
We Believe that Law Enforcement Can Best Be Achieved by
the Local Authorities, Complete Segregation with Equal
Facilities, No New Taxes, a Balanced Budget, Reduction of

State Debt, the Independence of the Legislature, Home Rule
for Local Authorities, Harmonious Labor-Management Relations, the Interests of Agriculture, Extra Pay to Firemen,
Increased Pay for Teachers, Undiminished Public Services,
Tourist Travel during the Summer Months (when it is
mighty hot), Bids on Contracts (this would be an innovation),
History and Traditions and the Continuation of the Algiers
and Gretna ferry services. The only things he acknowledged
opposing were Juvenile Delinquency and Subversion.

The Rainach advertisement, unlike the others, emphasized
an issue rather than a candidate. The art was freehand and
showed two dainty female children, the puffed skirts of their
crisp frocks midway up their plump thighs, picking flowers
that looked like daffodils from dandelion plants in the deep
shade of a spreading tree with the silhouette of a bunch of
celery. One little girl kneeled and culled, a frilly bit of the
bottom of her panties innocently peeping from beneath the
skirt, and turned a precociously provocative face toward her
sister, who stood and held the basket. There was a carefully
planted suggestion of eligibility for rape. The copy read:

> This is a fight to curb Louisiana's disastrous financial poli-
> cies. This is a fight to preserve States' Rights. This is a fight
> to protect the individual rights of the laboring man [*i.e.,*
> restore a right-to-work anti-union bill repealed by the Long
> legislature] and a fight to return Home Rule to our towns
> and parishes. But even more than that, THIS IS A FIGHT FOR
> OUR CHILDREN! WE CANNOT . . . WE *MUST* NOT leave them a
> heritage of integration to struggle against! WE MUST DO FOR
> THEM WHAT THEY CANNOT DO FOR THEMSELVES. Senator Rain-
> ach has led our fight for us for five years—when those whose

DUTY it was to lead refused because it might have hurt them
politically. He is the ONE candidate with the determination,
the will and the ability to turn back Northern Radicals and
the NAACP. FOR THE SAKE OF OUR CHILDREN, we *MUST* elect
Willie Rainach Governor! Elect the entire Rainach ticket.

The names and numbers followed.

A consolation was that Rainach had no chance. Louisiana
politics for nearly forty years had been a contest between
Longites and antis, with the Longites in favor of a welfare
state, soaking the oil companies and sharing the spoils.

The anti-Longites, at first battling to return the state to its
hereditary owners—themselves—had given up on that; they
now fought chiefly to lick the Longs and get a share of the
gravy, as in Britain the Tories, with no hope of restoring a
respectful pre-Labour Britain, declare themselves the party
of the Average Man and concentrate on winning office.

This followed a pattern set by the great Huey. If in the
beginning of his revolution he had followed other Southern
demagogues and attacked the Negro, his opponents would
have had to outbid him by attacking Negroes even more
violently. He had no need of the race issue; white poverty and
the backwardness of the state gave him all the ammunition
he needed. He adopted a policy of speaking disrespectfully of
Negroes in public to guard against being called a nigger lover,
and giving them what they wanted, under the table, to make
sure they would vote for him. As the poorest Louisianians
of all, they benefited disproportionately from his welfare
schemes; it would be a dull politician who would try to disfranchise his own safest voters.

Earl inherited and emphasized this policy, and Morrison,

starting in New Orleans, where the Negro vote is important, competed for it. To be fair to both, Earl genuinely liked Negroes—and for all I know, Huey did, too—while Morrison believes in their rights. Both were inevitablists and shrewd in the law.

Morrison sees no chance of stemming the tide of Federal court decisions. He suffers under the disadvantage of living in the contemporary world, while the Perezes and Rainachs remain in the Jurassic. It was the gift of the Longs that they could straddle the intervening million years.

The Davis people were working through the Old Regulars to round up all the Negro vote they could in New Orleans. Peace and harmony was their war cry.

Davis, to sum up, had the support of the big money men who need a winner, the *"element"* of gamblers and the local sheriffs who live off them; the *Times-Picayune* with its boiled shirt of respectability; the Old Regulars with their aura of venality; and a mass, hard to estimate, of upcountry people who like peace and hillbilly music.

Morrison had his own highly efficient New Orleans organization, all of French Catholic South Louisiana (except Plaquemines and St. Bernard, where Perez's authority overrides sectarian considerations), and the idealistic good-government people, earnest amateurs, with whom he had become a habit and reason for political life. These last formed a strong corps of volunteer workers. Noe and Dodd between them had the dyed-in-the-wool Longites, estimated by experts at a constant 40 per cent of the state vote. This was an overestimate. The Longites needed a Long to head their ticket, not merely to grace it.

These promised to be the three largest divisions of the electorate, and they turned out to be so, though not in the order or the proportions most observers expected. The racists were the smallest of all the factions.

That evening Tom Sancton and I listened to Jimmy Noe and Earl on WNOE, the Noe station.

"Chep Morrison is one of the ten bes'-dressed men in America," Noe said, "and Jimmie Davis hasn't got a backbone as big as a jellyfish. Ah'm pretty well fixed now, but as a young man ah pulled a cross-cut saw for fifty cents a day and wrestled an oil rig for a dollar and a half. It's an honor for me to pay my taxes. We stand for the people, the common people, the working man, the working woman, and if you don't elect us, *you will be the loser*. Who is the opposition? The old anti-Long crowd, the *Picayune* crowd. Huey Long was killed by newspaper persecution." This was the argument, familiar to all his hearers, that the newspapers had inflamed the assassin. "The same old crowd is here to fool you into throwing away the things Huey Long fought for. It's the same line they used when they fooled you into electing Sam Jones Governor in 1940. They couldn't elect Jones *dogketcher* today."

Uncle Earl, when he came in, said Governor Noe was a disinterested gentleman and had one of the best-raised families it had ever been his pleasure to meet.

"Vote for a candidate that the *Picayune* knows they can't tell what to do," he said. "They want to tell you what to do and what not to do, and they don't care which of those two sapsuckers, Morrison or Davis, gets elected."

Noe's speech sounded as if he had been away from politics too long and was still talking in 1940, and Earl sounded good-humored and perfunctory.

Next day, the date of the election, Sancton and I made a round of assorted precincts, or polling places. The approaches to them for a block in either direction were adorned with placards bearing candidates' photographs—a true Lebanese touch—and around the polls beribboned and besashed ladies on undertakers' chairs handed out sample ballots. There were, I think, two hundred and eleven names on the voting machine in most precincts, and to vote a complete Jimmie Davis—R.D.O. ticket in any ward a voter had to pull fifteen levers.

In addition to the sedentary ladies, there were roving, and in a surprising number of cases limping, males, to support challenged voters who appeared well-disposed. There were also flocks of small boys, who, however, appeared unreliable, like other irregular troops. The gutters leading up to most polls were deep in sample ballots, and so were the apertures to the mailboxes.

Morrison and Davis workers showed en masse, the Morrison watchers looking like virtuous dilettantes, the Davis people like Tammany block leaders. But in two precincts out of three there was nobody at all for Noe and Long, Rainach or Dodd. A political organization cannot be improvised: you either have to build one yourself, like Morrison, or rent a going one for the occasion, as the Davis people had chartered the R.D.O.

Down in Comiskey's ward the Davis ballots were going like

Clocker Lawton cards at the races. In a couple of mainly colored precincts where Tom stopped the station wagon, the voters were providing themselves with sample ballots of both kinds, to maintain the mystery.

When the poll-hopping palled, we drove back downtown to Curley's gym and watched a visiting colored fighter spar against a couple of local hopes, who began by trying to knock him out and then held like grim death. There were bleachers on two sides of the ring, one for white, one for colored, and, naturally, only colored inside the ropes. We got to talking with white old-timers there about when the color line invaded boxing in Louisiana.

As in other forms of race relations, there has been regression. In 1892, George Dixon, illustrious in history as Little Chocolate, fought Jack Skelly, an Irishman from Yonkers, for the featherweight championship of the world in New Orleans, and the mixed match was taken as a matter of course. None of the old-timers remembered when the color line came in. Over a long period relations improve slowly; then, very rapidly, they get a lot worse.

In 1872 there was a public meeting between fifty white and fifty Negro leaders, as equals, in New Orleans to discuss civil rights. Many of the white leaders were ex-Confederates. One was General Beauregard, whose committee report "advocated complete political equality for the Negro, an equal division of State offices between the races, and a plan whereby the Negroes would become landowners. It denounced discrimination because of color in hiring laborers or in selecting directors of corporations, and called for the abandonment of segregation in public conveyances, public places, railroads, steamboats and public schools."*

You couldn't get a leading Louisiana white to such a meeting now without a subpoena, and Beauregard, the Confederate Bonaparte, would be charged today with sabotaging the "Southern way of life."

The afternoon wore on, and toward sundown I made another tour of polling places, this time with Lacombe, the Neutral Corner's candidate for Governor; we used the Jefferson Downs Volkswagen. The lines in the working-class wards were heavy with men and women voting on their way home. Saloons were open, supposititiously for the sale of beer only. Bottles on the back bars were ostentatiously covered with newspaper. The Black Cat diminished as I watched. The dream was coming to an end. The polls closed at seven.

"I'm going to await the returns with my faithful workers at the Neutral Corner," he said. I wondered where else a man could have so much fun for $210, especially when another fellow put it up.

The result of the first primary was an upset. Morrison won handily.

The Morrison people had set up an election headquarters in a suite of two big banquet rooms off the mezzanine of the Sheraton-Charles, with wall charts on which to write the parish returns as they came in, television screens, Scotch and canapés and the rest of election-party paraphernalia. By about eleven o'clock, when Tom and I arrived, after a leisurely dinner and a bottle of Smith-Haut Lafitte 1947 at Arnaud's,

* T. Harry Williams, *P. G. T. Beauregard: Napoleon in Gray*. Louisiana State University Press, 1955.

the atmosphere was hopeful but scared, as I remembered it had been at radio parties in New York in the Truman-Dewey election of 1948. It was not only that Morrison was running as well as had been expected in the city, but that the other four candidates were cutting each other up in a manner that the Morrison faction had not dared hope for. People kept reminding one another that the returns from the country districts were not in yet.

The partisans at the Sheraton-Charles were predominantly scrubbed, well dressed and earnest, with the look of the dilettante in politics who feels he or she is doing a civic duty. Some of the women, steadying their nerves with whiskey, were already a trifle high. It was the kind of group that seldom has a winner, politics being what they are, and that is almost as astonished as pleased when it gets one.

Typically it is attracted to candidates like Willkie or Stevenson, or, on a municipal level, Bob Merriam in Chicago and Newbold Morris in New York. When it gets a consistent winner like La Guardia or Franklin D. Roosevelt it loses part of its regard for him. It is then obvious that its taste is shared by a large number of less discriminating people, and that devalues the candidate.

Morrison had been elected Mayor so often that he might have suffered from this prejudice, if he had not failed so dismally when he ran against Earl Long for Governor in 1956. That reinstated him.

As the evening wore on, no doubt survived that Morrison was in. In Orleans Parish, where in 1956 he had beaten Uncle Earl by barely 2,000 votes, he led all the four other serious candidates combined. He led Davis easily. The R.D.O., which had gathered 69,000 votes for Earl in 1956, had been able to get Davis only 40,000. Morrison took a lead of 46,000 upstate with him, and although he lost in many parishes outside, it was to different rivals in different places. On the whole he held his lead over Davis, and as the morning went on he increased it.

As the returns came in, a man named Paul McIlheny, a fervid Morrison buff, jotted down the votes for Big Bad Bill Dodd as regularly as the Mayor's and lumped the two totals. Then he would compare them with the total for the other three candidates. Dodd had already made his deal to throw in with Morrison for the runoff.

Dodd, unfortunately, was running badly, and watching McIlheny's honest distress, you would have thought he was Dodd's brother. The returns showed Willie Rainach running, I thought, surprisingly well, a not-too-distant third, but Tom said that the racists had expected even more. The great blow to me was Earl's showing. He was running far ahead of Jimmy Noe, his principal, and the Rainach and Dodd candidates for Lieutenant Governor, but he would fall far short of making the runoff. His effort to pick a soft touch had failed, and he was going to be shut out by a pair of four-round politicians.

About midnight Tom and I walked over to the Davis headquarters at the Hotel Monteleone, where there was considerable gloom. They had not yet lost the war, but they had lost a battle and would have to dicker for reinforcements. The Davis combination would now have to retain Willie Rainach, and possibly Uncle Earl, to help in the stretch.

When a political side becomes all-inclusive, there isn't enough gravy to go around.

Practical politics is like pari-mutuel betting: with everybody on the same horse, the payoff is small. Worse, the *Times-Picayune* was the keystone of the odd construction, and might hedge. Should it decide on a gesture in favor of unity, it might suggest editorially that the party waive the runoff and nominate Morrison unanimously, now that Earl Long, for once, was beaten out of the picture.

"If they do that, Chep will be more powerful than Huey was," Tom said. "He'll have state and city patronage both, plus a favorable national press. He can put in a safe Mayor here when he goes to Baton Rouge and leave a safe man in Baton Rouge as Governor while he goes on to the Senate in Washington. It will be a thousand-year Reich."

Tom sees things big and dramatically.

"There's no limit to his energy or his ambition," he said, "and he might turn out to be not only the first Catholic President of the United States—if Kennedy doesn't make it this time—but the first President from a Southern state since the Civil War. He's only forty-eight, and he walks on the water. Earl was the only one that could handle him. Now that Earl is out of the way, the genie is out of the bottle. Earl was the stopper."

We decided to return to the happier mood of the Sheraton-Charles and stopped for coffee at Thompson's on the way. There we encountered Blaise, too sensitive to show at the Neutral and be needled about his predicament that Davis would win.

"Morrison preys on da nigger vote and da woman vote," he said, and pretended he had business down the street.

At a table across the room, Tom pointed out Rainach, two children, his wife, and three or four members of his *Oberkommando*. All except the children, who seemed merely sleepy, looked down at the mouth.

"This marks the beginning of a new era in Louisiana politics," Tom said. Then I went to bed.

CHAPTER XII

BACK TO RACISM

When I awoke, I had a feeling of sadness, and could not remember why until I recognized my surroundings. Then I knew it was because I had come back to Louisiana to see Earl play Foxy Grandpa and run rings around the righteous, and he hadn't done it. From the time I had first heard his voice on a sound track in a television studio in New Orleans and seen him on the screen, wagging his tail and shaking his fist, I had liked the old stump-wormer.

I could still hear him saying to Willie Rainach with the Confederate flag on his tie: ". . . *you got to recognize that niggers is human beings.* . . . To keep fine honorable gray-headed men and women off the registration rolls, some of whom have been voting as much as sixty or sixty-five years—I plead with you in all candor. I'm a candidate for Governor. If it hurts me, it will just have to hurt."

The law that Earl had been attacking then allows any two registered bona fide voters of a parish to challenge any name on the voting list because of irregularity in the voter's original application. A misspelled name, an omitted initial or an error in calculating age *to the day* is sufficient. The parish registrar then "segregates the name"—always that verb. The challenged voter—if he gets the notification the registrar is legally obliged to send him, if he can read the notification (literacy per se is not a requisite for voting), if he cares enough to gather three witnesses to the legality of the first registration, if he can afford to pay a lawyer, and if he has guts enough to buck intimidation for the sake of a useless protest—may ask a hearing before the registrar. At this hearing he will be asked to reestablish his fitness to vote by answering impossible questions.

Rainach, as chairman of the Joint Legislative Committee on Segregation, was encouraging members of the White Citizens' Council and the Southern gentlemen in each parish to push the right of challenge to its ultimate length against Negroes.

The Department of Justice had brought action against white citizens of Washington Parish, on the Mississippi Line, for cutting 1,377 (out of 1,500) Negro voters from the list, and the case was before a Federal District Judge born, bred and legally trained in New Orleans, who, in due time, would order Washington Parish to restore the names to the rolls.

(I don't remember reading, in any of the voluminous accounts in Northern and Southern newspapers of Uncle Earl's uncouth conduct in the Legislature, any praise for the justice of his stand. In the dictionary of newspaper prejudices, which is seldom revised, Long was still a name of fun and fear.)

But the old boy was in there slugging, in a period when the accredited Southern liberals, of the kind exhibited at Wash-

ington dinner tables, talked about something else every time
civil rights was mentioned. Kefauver tried to weaken the
Senate bill on voting rights, and Fulbright filibustered
against it.

And I remembered his gift for prose: "You know the Bible
says that before the end of time, billy goats, tigers, rabbits,
and house cats all are going to sleep together," and "If you
give me the right commissioners, I can make them voting
machines play 'Home Sweet Home.' " You also need workers
at the polls to tell the voters what chords to hit, as he probably
realized by now.

I called the Hotel Roosevelt, where he stayed in New
Orleans, and when the desk said he had checked out, I tried
the Executive Mansion at Baton Rouge, where a state trooper
said he had not arrived. The old sapsucker was licking his
wounds, I imagined, and went back to sleep.

My telephone rang after a while. It was Tom Sancton, of
the opinion that we should drive up to Baton Rouge in his
station wagon and force our way in on our hero. "Once you
get to him he'll talk," Tom said. "It's his nature. He can't re-
sist." Tom is the old-fashioned kind of reporter who believes
in giving every story the old college try. I was against it, but
I had no other suggestion for what to do on Sunday.

Waiting for him, I read a Sunday newspaper that had been
printed before I went to bed. It had Morrison leading by
46,000 votes at 12:25.

We left in the early afternoon and were on the porch of
the Mansion in Baton Rouge in two hours. In the driveway
I had left crowded in early August, there was only one car
parked besides Tom's.

I was sorry for the poor old Governor, abandoned by the
Old Regulars, alienated from his wife, held at the other end
of a telephone wire by his favorite woman friend, and so surrounded by snooping newspaper reporters that he could not
even peacefully enjoy a visit with a strip-tease girl. He was
alone, but without enough privacy to cover up a red bug.

I was astonished, when I went inside, to be told by the
state cop on the door that the Governor wasn't available because he was closeted with Camille Gravel, the Democratic
National Committeeman from Louisiana, a leading Morrison
manager. The last time I had seen Long and Gravel together,
in Alexandria, Gravel's home town, they had been jawing
each other at close range in public. Earl had called Gravel a
common damn hoodlum and a little pissant, and Gravel had
called Earl a doublecrosser and a lifelong liar.

I asked the cop to send in word that I, the Governor's great
and loyal admirer from New York, was there, having driven
up from New Orleans to condole with him. The cop said the
Governor had instructed he wasn't seeing *anybody,* but he sent
in word. After a while, a colored man came out from the direction of the conference and said the Governor said to run me
away from there.

I promptly sent Tom to look for Margaret Dixon. His departure gave me a stay of sentence. Even the most inhuman
official will not chuck you out *on foot.* In our country the
thought of pedestrian locomotion is so abhorrent that even a
policeman who would gladly beat you up would be ashamed
to make you walk. It is the twentieth-century equivalent of
dropping a man at sea in an oarless rowboat.

In the Tunisian steppe, I knew an infantry company, brave

under fire, that quailed at the notion of moving to a new position five miles away on foot. It stayed where it was for twenty-four hours after receiving the order to move, waiting for trucks to come and move it. The division commander, when he heard about it, said, "Why can't the goddam infantry walk?" His harshness led to a Congressional inquiry.

Tom had just departed when the door from the library, where the conference was in session, opened, and a young lawyer I had met in New Orleans came out and spotted me. He was in politics, like everybody else, and, as is natural for an energetic young liberal in the Great State, was a Morrison man. (Energy and liberalism are both used in a regional, or relative, sense.) I hailed him and asked if the Governor and Gravel were still calling each other names, and he said no, they had business to attend to. I asked him to intercede with Earl and get me an audience, and he said he would try. I did not see him again that day.

The cop said to stand on the porch, as the Governor was in a hell of a temper. He shunted me out on the porch that the *State Guide* calls a colonnaded portico. I stood there thinking of all the important people who had been *glad* to receive me in other days: Pola Negri and Henry Luce and Joe Louis and the two fellows who wrote "The Music Goes Round and Round." The list is endless. Now I had fallen so low that I couldn't get in to see a defeated candidate for Lieutenant Governor of Louisiana. After a while, Tom drove up with the gracious Mrs. Dixon, but it was no good. The troopers turned all three of us away. Mrs. Dixon, fresh from the teletypes in the *Advocate* office, said Morrison's final lead looked to be about 65,000.

As Tom and I drove back down to New Orleans later, he said, "That's Earl for you, every time: In victory unbearable, insufferable in defeat."

He still thought Morrison sure. "Earl wouldn't be sweet-talking Gravel if he didn't think so too," he said. After being up all night listening to the returns, Maggie said, Chep was out stumping at noon. He held the first meeting of his campaign for the runoff election today at New Roads, on False River, the town where he was born.

At this point in my narrative, my hero, Earl Kemp Long, was in the side pocket.

By the time we sat down to dinner in New Orleans—three dozen apiece at Felix's and then shrimp and crabmeat Arnaud and red snapper *en court bouillon*—the early editions of the *Times-Picayune*, with all but complete returns and tabulations, were on the street. Morrison had about 272,000 votes; Davis 210,000; Rainach 138,000; poor Jimmy Noe 96,000; and Big Bad Bill 86,000 (the two Long factions between them 182,000). Rainach, although third, represented only the fourth biggest segment of the electorate. For Lieutenant Governor, Morrison's running mate, Bowdon, had about 223,000 votes, Davis's man, Aycock, 215,000, and Uncle Earl 156,000. He had run wretchedly in New Orleans, where he had lost the services of the Old Regular Organization.

Morrison had carried five congressional districts out of eight, including not only New Orleans and Baton Rouge, but all rural southern Louisiana. Davis had carried only two districts, in northwest Louisiana. In the remaining one, the Fourth, which included Davis's home city of Shreveport and Rainach's rustic constituency of Claiborne, Willie had topped the poll, getting more than Davis and Morrison combined.

It gave one to think, and Davis's managing directors clearly had thought.

The editorial page, on which the Morrison rooters had hoped to see a flag of truce, talked instead of a hard-fought second primary, pointing out that Morrison had 33 per cent of the vote, Davis 25 and Rainach 17. "The disposition of the Rainach voters, numbering nearly 140,000, will be of more than slight importance."

More interesting than the statistics was Davis's statement. Peace and harmony had gone out the window with his failure to cut into Morrison's Negro vote.

"There has been one sinister and disturbing element injected into this election," said the Sunshine man, "which is clearly apparent after an analysis of the precincts in the state dominated by the minority elements." Any Southerner knows that "minority" is the plural of "nigger."

"My personal conviction coupled with the overwhelming vote of confidence placed in Mr. Jack P. F. Gremillion, who has been re-elected Attorney General, confirms my faith that the voters of this state are concerned with the preservation of State Rights as guaranteed by the Tenth Amendment to the Constitution of the United States." This paragraph was set in blackface.

"The Vote that has been cast in this first primary has proven several points. One is that the majority of the voters in Louisiana want to preserve state sovereignty and the right to self-determination in internal matters.

"The second point that has been graphically established is that there are forces at work that will undermine, by tactics fair or foul, the rights of an overwhelming majority of citizens."

These forces, of course, are the Communist party and the Elders of Zion, of whose fornications the NAACP is a byblow, as any initiated grass-eater knows. Grass-eater was Earl Long's term for the race nuts. Davis was now talking their language, and the violence of 1960 was in the making.

The act of the Louisiana legislature creating the Rainach committee begins: "Whereas, the rights and liberties of the people of the United States are threatened as never before by enemies, both foreign and domestic; and

"Whereas, these enemies have concentrated their attacks upon the States in the South and are there employing what has been described by these enemies as the Party's most powerful weapon—racial tension; . . ."

Back to Davis: "I will campaign on this mandate. This, coupled with the genuine record established during the time I served the people as Governor, and underscored by my platform for the future, will lead to an inevitable victory at the polls in the second primary election." He was, in the elegant language of politics, sucking up to the grass-eaters.

In the column adjoining the second half of the statement, the *Times-Picayune* make-up man had thoughtfully placed an item on Camille Gravel, re-elected to the Democratic State Committee. A paragraph in blackface type read:

"Gravel, 45, said the vote gave him the right to speak up as a 'segregation moderate.'

"While he hasn't made a public endorsement, Gravel is backing the gubernatorial bid of deLesseps Morrison."

I said to Tom, "It reads like Arkansas. It's going to be a

White Supremacy election. But in Little Rock at least they had a newspaper with guts, the *Arkansas Gazette,* that resisted the regression. The *Times-Picayune* is pushing this one on."

We were not in a truly merry mood when after dinner we headed for the Neutral Corner (White) to congratulate Lacombe on his showing. The chart by parishes in the paper showed he had gathered 4,895 votes for Governor, finishing a hot seventh. He had got 292 votes in New Orleans and been skunked in only two parishes out of 64. His best totals were in a number of Cajun parishes that he had never visited. He had the most clearly French name on the program.

"We murdered them in Echo!" the candidate said, triumphant.

"Where are you going to throw your support in the run-off, Allen?" Tom asked him.

"I have already endorsed Chep Morrison," the recent candidate said. "There is a job at the city jail I have my eye on."

Blaise squeaked with joy. "The Black Cat never picked a winner in his life," he said. "Now the ele*ment* can ozoom Davis is elected."

By Tuesday, when I flew back to New York, the two survivors of the first primary were squared away on the last leg. The *Times-Picayune* reported:

NAACP TARGET OF DAVIS TALK

In Louisiana this is as safe as opposing incest.

" 'As for the NAACP, I hope not one of them votes for me because I don't want their vote,' " the candidate was quoted.

"He referred to the National Association for the Advancement of Colored People."

" 'I'm not a hater but there comes a time when you must stand on your principles,' Davis added. 'We know what is good for the country and we don't want someone from New York running our state.' "

Meanwhile poor Morrison, in a town called Raceland, was disclaiming ever having a kind thought about anybody with less than 32 quarterings of Norman albino blood. He said he had taken "vigorous positive action to maintain segregation," but he spoiled it by saying that in fighting the NAACP "I have used my head instead of my mouth."

The mouth is the traditional weapon. Some great author should write a companion volume to Cash's classic *The Mind of the South*. It would be called *The Mouth of the South*.

Vainly, I felt, though accurately, Morrison denounced Davis for "the overnight change of heart that prompted him to finally make a statement on the issue."

The Negro-inhabited precincts had voted for *him,* and that was as fatal as having your social standing vouched for by Elsa Maxwell.

I felt, too, that there was an out-of-date look about Morrison's quoted plea that he had "met this problem successfully because he 'provided through vigorous action and timely performance adequate and equal opportunities and facilities for the 235,000 Negroes in New Orleans.' "

The grass-eaters consider "adequate and equal" a sign of softness. "Vigorous" is another word that Morrison uses too often. It has connotations of hard labor that displease voters in a warm climate.

"Aggressive," which has associations with violence, goes down better.

In the lobby of the Sheratonized St. Charles, I met the lawyer I had seen at the Mansion on Sunday, and he said that Earl had promised to come down to New Orleans and confer with Morrison but had not appeared.

"The Davis people must have got to him between Sunday night and Monday morning," he said mournfully. And Morrison, by going campaigning early on Sunday, had missed a chance to make an offer to Rainach.

Davis's people, rising late, had seen him first. Vigor can be a vice.

By now the *States-Item*, the *Times-Picayune* Company's afternoon coda, bragged the first primary as, on the main issue, a resounding *Times-Picayune* victory. Its lead editorial on Monday was headed "Longism Takes a Beating," and began: "Last Saturday's voting left many important nominations still to be made in a Democratic runoff primary, but on that Louisiana political phenomenon called Longism the action was decisive.

"Gov. Earl K. Long, seeking the Lieutenant Governor's post, and his handpicked candidate for governor, James A. Noe, were eliminated from further consideration.

"Unless one of the two surviving tickets in the second primary becomes prominently identified with the Long faction, the perennial choice between Longism and anti-Longism will not be the paramount issue of the runoff.

"That is a development for which the voters can rejoice. It is heartening to realize that other factors, other reasons, will bear more heavily on the runoff choice. . . ."

The "other factors, other reasons," that were to "bear more heavily on the runoff choice," were racism and the denial of civil rights—"the segregation cause."

The result reminded me of one of those automobile accidents in which a driver, swatting at a wasp, loses control of his car and runs it into a bayou full of alligators. The sequel was to prove that the *Times-Picayune*, in its eagerness to get rid of the Governor, had helped move Louisiana back into the class of Alabama.

CHAPTER XIII

EARL JOINS *TIMES-PIC*

I had a chance to study the alligators in the plane on the way back to New York. Stopping by the Rainach campaign headquarters on the day before election, I had picked up a batch of literature that I had neither time nor taste for reading in New Orleans, but the boredom of the air lends itself to catching up on distasteful homework.

The windows of the Rainach store front on Union Street had been pasted over with blow-ups and reproductions of newspaper pages denouncing Davis for having led his orchestra in a drive-in dance place in California where Negroes were allowed on the same floor with Whites, and for having later himself managed an "interracial honky-tonk" of the same sinister nature in Palm Springs. But these sins of youth were to be forgiven in view of Willie Rainach's own defeat and Davis's promise to mend his ways.

The first article of indictment against Morrison that I read was a throwaway headed

MORRISON WORKS TO DESTROY SEGREGATION

Under this head was a photograph of the Mayor between two well-dressed colored men. Under that was another photo, of a number of Negro boys diving into a swimming pool surrounded by massed Negroes, some of whose faces and bodies looked white in the glare of the photographer's flashlight. No form of reporting lends itself better than the camera to equivocation.

A caption read: "The above picture was taken from the Saturday July 31, 1948 LOUISIANA WEEKLY, a New Orleans Negro Newspaper.

"In the course of his speech dedicating the Negro swimming pool shown in the above picture, the *Louisiana Weekly* quoted Mayor Chep Morrison as having said that he *'plans for full integration of the Negro community in expanding the educational and recreational program of New Orleans. . . .'*" The word "integration" did not pick up its additional special sense until after the United States Supreme Court's school decision of 1954, when it began to be used as an antonym of "segregation." Morrison's 1948 "integrate" meant, as in the dictionary, "to fit in as a harmonious part," under the old "equal and adequate" scheme:

"Facts from the record reveal that Mayor Chep Morrison urged upon leading New Orleans Hotels to register Negroes; that he attended the testimonial banquet for the Negro lawyer Tureaud who represented the NAACP in all their suits to force racial integration in our public schools, colleges and LSA;

"That as a member of the Board of Directors of the Pelican

Baseball Team, he advocated measures which would 'de-segrate' the Pelican Baseball Stadium as well.

"The only streetcars and buses in the State of Louisiana which are racially integrated are those in New Orleans, under Mayor Chep Morrison."

Before I came to Louisiana, I would have thought all these statements recommendations for Mayor Morrison's good sense. Such is the force of conditioning, even in two brief visits, that I now sought to find mitigating circumstances to explain each. Morrison, not wanting the city to be boycotted as a site for national conventions, had asked the hotels to lodge Negro delegates to some of them. He had felt that the Pelicans needed new strength and the patronage of Negro fans in order to survive. (Failing on both counts, the Pelicans perished.)

It was true, I knew, that a Federal court had ordered the Orleans Parish School Board to produce a plan for the ad-mission of Negro pupils to the same schools as whites. The plan had to be brought into court by the end of the current school year, and a whole new cycle of litigations would then begin, the judge defining what he would accept as a minimum of compliance with the law, the Board trying to whittle down the minimum. I felt sure, too, that Morrison knew that the court's order could not be completely evaded with-out shutting down all the schools, and, since he himself was intelligent, I assumed he preferred that schools remain open. I could not believe, though, that he had initiated a plot to force the School Board's hand. (I would have liked him better if he had.)

Before reading the White League's offering, I had been on

the fence about Morrison. The White League converted me
to his side. It seemed hard that a man should be punished
precisely for his best point.

Davis, merely negative before the election, now was the
White League's color-bearer.

I spent part of the rest of my short journey reading another
piece of White League documentation: "Three Steps to Mongrelization—A Blueprint for the Destruction of Our Christian-
American Civilization. The Three Steps are: 1. Mix the
schools—Their immediate goal is the integration of the
schools; their ultimate objective is the bastardization of the
white race; 2. Teach Them 'Tolerance'—The second important step toward total mongrelization is the indoctrination
of our white youth with 'tolerance' propaganda; 3. Integrate
the Churches—a project dear to the heart of a great many of
our social gospel clergymen. They know to begin with the
mere presence of Negroes in white churches will eventually
result in interracial marriages."

The tract was illustrated with smudgy photos of mixed
couples: "This girl, on honeymoon with her Negro husband,
will make her parents proud some day—with mulatto grandchildren," one caption said.

By the time I reached home I thought that Morrison's
campaign in Louisiana might be a watershed in Southern
history. If the Mayor, a Catholic and a realist, could win,
intimidated liberals and moderate-liberals might take heart
throughout the South, which is not monolithically insane.

The grass-eaters like to say of militant Negroes that the
majority are prisoners of a few thousand who force the
others to conform by threats. The *Colons* say the same of the

Algerians, and the Afrikanders of the Africans. It is more true of Southern whites then of any other group.

A Senator as ostentatiously civilized as Fulbright of Arkansas abstained from battle against Governor Orval Faubus in his own state, telling friends in Washington that it were better he knuckle under than that Arkansas be represented in the United States Senate by a troglodyte like Faubus himself. This was in 1957, and Fulbright was not due to face the electorate until 1962. The Senator was so sure that independence would be fatal that he quit five years early.

On the morning I left New Orleans the *Times-Picayune* carried the announcement that the Morrison supporters had expected: "Dodd Declares for Morrison," but it was a question of how many of the 86,000 votes Dodd had collected in the first primary he would be able to deliver. The Dodd voters, for the most part, were upstate, living among the Davis and Rainach voters, and the "new issues" were bound to appeal to them, especially if the newspapers continued to advertise Morrison's Negro vote.

A *Times-Picayune* I bought at the out-of-town newsstand in New York shortly after arriving carried a first-page story on the slightly increased registration in New Orleans for the runoff. Part of the headline read: "2262 more Negroes on Roll; 1087 Whites." A paragraph, the only one in the story that was printed in blackface type, reprised:

"The new total represents net increases of 2262 in the number of Negroes registered and of only 1087 in the number of White persons on the rolls."

This could be translated into a clear indication that the Negroes, for dark reasons of their own, were out to elect

Morrison, but in order that not even the dullest should miss the point, the paper added:

"In the first primary, Mayor deLesseps S. Morrison, among the candidates for Governor, received the overwhelming majority of the Negro vote in New Orleans and state-wide."

There were about 150,000 Negro voters registered in the state, as compared with 850,000 whites. In New Orleans there were 34,000 (including the sinister accretion) and 170,000 whites. Negroes comprise about 24 per cent of the state's population, and the discrepancy between this and their 15 per cent of state-wide registration reflects in part the obstacles thrown in their way to the polls. It reflects in other part an apathy founded on skepticism.

With only two men running, Davis could turn the Negroes' adherence to Morrison into an asset, and the *Times-Picayune* and the Shreveport *Times* did all they could to exaggerate it.

A Louisiana election is fun to watch even from New York. Thus Bill Dodd, who before the first primary had said, "Chep Morrison got soft little hands like a girl's," now told a crowd:

"I'm a hillbilly from up North Louisiana, where the people are going to vote for Chep Morrison just like you folks down here are going to vote for him.

"Chep Morrison is as far ahead of Jimmie Davis as a rocket is ahead of a mule. One is a fighter and the other is a fiddler—now which do you want?

"One of them will do something, and the other will do nothing. Now which do you want? If you want nothing you got nothing running for Governor—Jimmie Davis!"

Davis stumped the state, spurning, in every speech, unproffered aid from the NAACP or the Teamsters' Union. He

wanted the votes of all decent people, he said every time.
"However, I have repeatedly said, and I say again, that I am
not accepting support of the NAACP, teamster's boss Jimmy
Hoffa, or that ilk." Back in 1947, when he was Governor, the
Times-Picayune had accused him editorially of kowtowing to
Hoffa during a strike. Now that counted no more than a base
hit in a different inning of some other ball game.

Going down to the Cajun country to attack Morrison in
his own stronghold, he carried with him a legislator named
Angelle, "who spoke in French." "Davis and his hillbilly band
entertained a crowd gathered at the Arcadia Parish courthouse at Crowley. He sang one number in French." It was
here that Davis again declared he wanted no part of the
NAACP and the Jimmy Hoffa Group.

"I have been criticized for saying that I do not want the
vote and support of the NAACP and the Jimmy Hoffa
crowd," Davis said, "but I will say again that I do not want
their help." I wondered who had criticized him.

Morrison said he was for segregation too. But then, why
had the Negroes voted for him? The answer, the newspapers
implied, was obvious to any white man who could recognize
a woodpile when he saw one.

"Ex.-Gov. Davis tried to give the impression during the
first primary that he was such a nice old soul who just loved
everybody and everything," Morrison said in a speech in a
place called Baker three days after the primary. "He was not
a hater, he said. . . .

"But the first words to come out of his mouth the day after
election carried the old practiced ring of all professional
haters—namely, the denunciation of minorities. . . .

"He didn't say one word in the three months of stumping prior to the first primary about segregation or states' rights.

"He made his livelihood for many years operating an integrated honky-tonk in California, yet now he says he is all for segregation and states' rights." (Davis later denied this story, first publicized by the Rainach people, who were soon to join him. Morrison, however, stuck to it.)

"Just who is he slurring now? Is he criticizing the Catholics of our State, or the Jews, or the Italians, or the Syrian communities scattered throughout Louisiana—or is he complaining about the good Cajuns, like myself, who, all over South Louisiana, saw through his peace and harmony pitch and voted for the Morrison-Bowdon ticket, which, to them, meant industry, progress and prosperity."

Editorials in both New Orleans papers attacked as disingenuous this attempt to twist the accepted Southern meaning of the word "minorities." Herman Deutsch, the dean of New Orleans columnists, said it was one of the things that had disillusioned him with the new Morrison, who had undergone a sinister metamorphosis since the day when the publishers changed their minds about him.

The newspaper with this speech in it brought also word that Jimmy Noe, Uncle Earl's candidate for Governor, had thrown in with the Mayor for the runoff. His long written statement lacked the Tabasco of spoken Louisianian, but it had its points.

"In truth and fact, Jimmie Davis is only a half-citizen of Louisiana, as his long residences in unsegregated California prove," Mr. Noe wrote, as if unsegregation were a contagious

itch and Mr. Davis ought to be quarantined and decontam-
inated before Louisiana was again exposed to him.

What bothered me about the story from Baker, though,
was the lead:

"Gubernatorial candidate Chep Morrison claimed last
night that Jimmie Davis, his opponent in the second primary,
has accepted the endorsement of Governor Earl K. Long.

" 'And don't pay any attention to any denials,' said Morrison. 'I know for a fact that Long has gone with Davis and
Davis has embraced him. . . .

" 'It's plain to see that all the discredited, disreputable
political machines in the state have gotten together behind
Davis in a frantic attempt to keep their hands in the political
trough.' " There is no animal that eats out of a trough with
its hands, I thought here, irrelevantly—but no matter.

"At the Governor's office in Baton Rouge," the paper inter-
polated, "a staff member said the Governor had informed
him, 'I have not endorsed anyone for Governor in the second
primary.' "

There is a shade between "I have not endorsed" and "I
have not agreed to endorse" that can save a man from telling
a lie.

I was sure that Morrison would not have made the charge
while any hope remained of landing Earl.

Bill White, who had run for Lieutenant Governor with
Dodd, was now working for Davis. (There is an old Hellenistic proverb: "Two hands in two troughs are better than one
hand in one trough.")

I was entertained but not convinced by an Associated Press
story describing Earl's detachment in defeat. "Earl K. Long is

taking life easy since his disastrous bid for the Democratic nomination as Lieutenant Governor," this one began. "Long is not in seclusion. But few can reach him.

"After the December 5 election, Long spent several days at his Winnfield farm—doing the things he loves most." Here I could picture him with a half acre of past-performance charts spread out before him as he played the races by telephone. "Once he was reported hunting wild hogs, perhaps his only active outdoor sport.

"When in the mood, the Governor and his workers, with horses and dogs, chase down the animals, bring them into pens and put them on a good diet to prepare them for butchering."

Combining direct and circumstantial evidence, I estimated that old Earl must have been signing up with Davis on the afternoon that the *States-Item* published its editorial "Longism Is Dead" and said voters could respect either of the runoff candidates providing he did not get mixed up with Long.

Rainach, meanwhile, kept as mum as Long. Davis continued to say there was no use side-stepping the fact that the NAACP had delivered a bloc vote to Morrison. The Mayor said that if Davis wanted to talk about bloc votes, he should talk about Plaquemines Parish, where District Attorney Leander H. Perez, racist and richest of oilmen, had "evolved a dictatorship that would make Khrushchev look like a piker."

Perez, operating in French Catholic territory, had created a solid Davis enclave in Morrison territory.

The counterattack had no effect. Perez's bloc was not a Negro bloc, although it included Perez's Negro vassals. In the

Times-Picayune's eyes, blocs *as* blocs were benign. The only malignant bloc was a bloc for Morrison.

"In Plaquemines, Perez has thrown the U.S. Constitution into the Mississippi River," Morrison said. "If I'm elected, we'll see some daylight and fresh air and freedom come back into Plaquemines."

That kind of talk was like giving Davis a blank check signed by Perez, I reflected regretfully. Morrison was losing his temper.

He lashed out at the gamblers, too, and this, I felt, remembering Blaise's talk of the *"element,"* was another mistake in the field of finance. (Forty-one sheriffs out of sixty-four declared for Davis before the runoff election date.)

The last ten days of the campaign saw a classic double envelopment of the Mayor's faction. Rainach gave Davis his official blessing on December 29. It was the extreme faction of the bug-eyed—of whom I shall exhibit a sample before this essay ends—that only Rainach in person could re-assure. As the battle loomed increasingly dubious, the value of the prophet's intervention rose. He secured as part of his price the promise of a spot to be created for him in the new administration that would keep him in the public eye for four years.

As a sober Associated Press dispatch on the first page of the *Times-Picayune* had it:

RAINACH BACKS DAVIS FOR POST

Shreveport, La.—Segregation chief William Rainach ended his long silence Friday and named former Governor Jimmie Davis as his candidate in the January 9 Democratic runoff for Governor.

The State Senator from Summerfield, head of the Joint

Legislative Committee on Segregation, said Davis made a
number of commitments on the segregation issue when the
two conferred two days ago.

(Common report also had it that he made a commitment to
reimburse the Senator for his first-primary campaign expenses, plus a substantial *pourboire*.)

Rainach, third man in the December 5 primary, was
critical of both Davis and New Orleans Mayor deLesseps
Morrison during the campaign. There were reports Rainach
might remain neutral during the runoff.

The Rainach statement said Davis, second to Morrison in
the first primary, agreed to support creation of a state sovereignty committee to handle states' rights and segregation
matters with Rainach as its head.

Rainach's old job as head of the legislative segregation
committee would go to Representative John Garrett of Claiborne Parish under the agreement with Davis, the statement
said.

Rainach had had to give up his Claiborne senate seat to
run for Governor in the first primary. Garrett, as Claiborne
member of the house, was presumably a trusty friend.

All other members of the committee would be reap-
pointed, and Garrett would have the right to fill vacan-
cies. . . .

The sovereignty commission would work across state lines,
Rainach's statement said, to form a Southern coalition to
fight the South's cause and conduct a national advertising
and public relations program to carry the South's story to
the North.

Camille Gravel of Alexandria, national Democratic com-

212   THE EARL OF LOUISIANA

mitteeman from Louisiana, is Morrison's chief political ad-
viser, Rainach's statement continued. Gravel is "close to Paul
Butler, national Democratic Chairman *and other Northern
radicals.*" [*Those* italics are mine.]

Gravel is also "closely tied to the NAACP bloc vote that
went unanimously to Morrison," the statement said.

Rainach has been in a Homer hospital since the first primary, in which he polled 143,500 votes.

The segregation prophet's stay in the hospital had been due
to depression and exhaustion from overwork, the same kind
of thing that hospitalized Earl in the spring that now seemed
ages ago. The newspapers did not suggest that he was crazy.

The Shreveport *Times,* up in Caddo Parrish, at the northern edge of the state, where Rainach had whipped Davis in
the first primary, published the speech of absolution in full,
four columns of close-set type. Here are a few paragraphs:

"I don't think there is anyone running for Governor among
the entire eleven—or anyone else in the State of Louisiana—
who would take as strong a stand as I would take, but I do
believe Jimmie Davis would take the next strongest stand in
the State of Louisiana.

"I know there have been a lot of rumors about Jimmie
Davis practicing integration in an integrated nightclub in
California. [His own organization had put them about.] We
had a detective agency to check Jimmie Davis for our own
satisfaction to see whether or not this was true.

"We had other reports from California running down
rumors about photographs [dancing with Lena Horne] and
so forth out there. And in all those reports we never found
that matters were as they had been reported.

"All of you saw a clipping—an ad that was run in the Shreveport *Journal* showing how Mayor Morrison got the NAACP bloc vote in New Orleans and Baton Rouge and other places in the state. It is listed by ward and precincts. It is unquestioned that he got the NAACP bloc vote in the first primary on December 5.

"On the other hand, Governor Davis has disowned the NAACP bloc vote in the state of Louisiana. He says he does not want it. He'll get elected Governor of the State of Louisiana without it.

"He also agreed to use interposition to interpose the sovereignty of the State of Louisiana, the police power of this state, to protect the people of this state from Federal oppression. He also told me that he will go to jail if necessary to protect the people of Louisiana from Federal oppression. . . .

"I am in a better position than others to judge the background of the candidates for Governor of Louisiana. I want to urge everyone to get out and get to the polls on January 9 to politic their neighbors for the Jimmie Davis ticket. . . ."

As to poor Morrison, Rainach said, "He has given ground to the NAACP in Federal courts in every instance of the city of New Orleans." In White League Citizen's Council language, an official obeying a court order obeys not the court or the Government of the United States, but the power *behind* the Government. This is of course the National Association for the Advancement of Colored People, an organ of the Soviet Union.

"He has denied that they have integration in the City of New Orleans. But I have here a clipping from the Shreveport *Times*—the same appeared in the *Times-Picayune*—dated

December 22, 1958, where they ended segregation in the New Orleans City Park and swimming pools and various and sundry other facilities in New Orleans City Park. . . .

"Mayor Morrison has also integrated the police force of the City of New Orleans—contemplating integrating the fireman force of the City of New Orleans."

There was nothing much Morrison could do about that, I knew. A man who let colored and white people walk in the same park was beyond political redemption in northern Louisiana, and to put Negroes on a force that Negroes paid taxes to support was the most inequitable proposition I could contemplate. (Headline: "Davis Welcomes Rainach Stand—Hails Success in Uniting Segregation Forces.")

The Governor ended *his* long silence a week later:

DAVIS GETS HIS VOTE, SAYS LONG

"Governor Earl K. Long Tuesday ended a month-long silence after his political defeat and said he will vote for former Governor Jimmie Davis in the Democratic runoff for Governor.

"The 64-year-old Long, looking rested and healthy, said he cast an advance absentee ballot for Davis Monday while in Winnfield, his home town." (Until he joined Davis, newspapers had invariably reported Earl looked gaunt, sick or fatigued.)

" 'The reason I'm voting for Mr. Davis,' " Long emphasized, " 'is that I think Mr. Davis is a kind man, a tolerant man, a Christian man, and I've always found him truthful—that means more to me than anything else.' " (Forgotten: "Davis loves money like a hog loves slop.")

" 'I don't believe Mr. Davis has any rancor or hatred toward any group—Italians, French, colored or anyone.'

"If he thought Davis would try to punish Catholics, Negroes, or anyone, Long said, 'I wouldn't vote for him.'

"In a suddenly announced press conference, Long said, 'It looks like the trend is for Davis. It looks like Davis has gained more in the last few days.' "

Then, like a practiced barroom fighter, he said the man he slugged had swung at him but missed.

"He called the news session, Long said, because Morrison, an old foe, 'has been saying I've been calling up people night and day and asking them to vote for Davis.'

" 'I've called a few friends, Mr. Morrison would be surprised how few.'

"Long avoided the terms 'endorsement' or 'support' in mentioning his vote for Davis.

"The Governor stressed that Davis didn't solicit his vote. He said he offered it immediately after the first primary. 'And I didn't ask Davis for as much as a soda cracker.' "

If Earl had indeed promised his "vote" to Davis before going up to Baton Rouge that Sunday, he had certainly fooled Gravel and his younger colleague in the afternoon. They came away thinking they had him half hooked.

I inclined to think he had not committed himself finally until the next day, after weighing both bids and giving the Davis people a chance to top the Morrison offer. Afterward I heard that he had been on the point of going on the stump for Morrison because he was so angry at Jim Comiskey and the Old Regulars for having let him down, but that he had telephoned to his estranged wife for counsel and she had

talked him out of it. Morrison and his late wife, with their
snooty city ways, had said things to rile Miz Blanche in previous campaigns, and she hadn't Earl's thick hide. Neither had
Morrison, for that matter; he had never forgiven Earl for
calling him "Dellasoups," and the old boy may have sensed
it. Davis, Earl probably felt, was a fellow he could handle
when the time came. Sunshine Jimmie had no personal organization like Morrison's Crescent City Democratic club.

"Oil has da best of both woilds," an old associate said
enviously when he saw the statement. "If elected, he gets
office, and defeated he gets money." But this was merely an
informed guess.

As to why Earl came in on the same side as "that little pinheaded nut, Willie Rainach," and the other grass-eaters, he
would have answered that if he stayed neutral, Davis would
probably win anyway. Then Perez and Rainach would have
full control of his policy. If Earl came in, he might speak for
sweet reason.

After all, the *Times-Picayune* was in there with Earl Long,
and the gamblers, Comiskey, and the race cranks. It was like
what he had once called a "Biblical proposition." Who was he
to be more saintly than the *Times-Picayune?*

CHAPTER **XIV**

WHO'S CRAZY NOW?

I read about the second rupture of silence, Earl's, the day before I returned to New Orleans to watch the final heat. The trip was becoming a habit. There was the same departure out of the overheated cattle shed at La Guardia, with the abutting fellow passengers' hand luggage jammed into kidney and groin, the same toothpaste-ad-smile welcome aboard the brand of jet that falls apart with cheery regularity when I am not flying, and the same dreadful airplane meal. I had, as always, a bundle of *Times-Picayune*s and Shreveport *Times*es to read on the way down—my homework.

Morrison was in there battling, as if "Invictus" were *his* house song instead of the Longs'. He had women's Morrison broom brigades organized among the Junior Leaguers to sweep corruption out of office, and schemes for multiplying oysters and breeding muskrats and building roads where they were needed in whatever part of the state he found himself campaigning. He had been saying all along that Earl and Davis

217

were in cahoots—a Davis administration would be "an Earl Long deal with a Davis front." In another art this is called riding a punch—getting in on it before it picks up snap.

"At Franklinton," a story of one Morrison meeting said, "Morrison displayed Jimmie Davis Song Books, in which he said were songs too filthy to quote in public. He said the chorus from a reported Davis song called 'Sewing Machine Blues' reads:

> " 'I'm going to telephone Heaven to send me an angel down,
>   But if they don't have any angels,
>   Then send me a high-stepping brown.' "

Now that Earl had broken silence, Chep said, the opposition was "caught red-handed in another lie—I have said it before and I repeat it again—all Earl Long needs is a weak-kneed, part-time Governor like Davis for him to continue running the state as he has for the past four years."

Instead of old Earl's "Biblical proposition" he called the consortium a jambalaya, a kind of Louisiana stew with everything in it but the kitchen stove: "We ask, isn't this a fine jambalaya, with Earl Long, the *Times-Picayune*, Leander Perez, the Shreveport *Times*, the Old Regulars, all together in one pot?"

But the odds appeared too great. He was like a man with a high pair on the deal who fails to draw, while the Davis combination had landed that third deuce. Davis had had 25 per cent of the vote on the first primary, and added to it was Rainach's 17 per cent—the segregation bit had done the trick. In Southern professional politics, it is known as "the black ace off the bottom of the deck." That gave him an edge over Morrison's 33 per cent of the first vote. Earl had certainly canceled out any influence Dodd and Noe may have had over the old Longites—that segment of the central and northern Louisiana rural mass that had learned under Huey to vote for its own stomach, without any flummery about the Southern way of life. Most Longites, with the encouragement of the hereditary Lama, would treat themselves this time to the luxury of a vote for prejudice. Dodd and Noe between them had drawn 21 per cent of the vote, and at least three quarters of that, I imagined, would now go to Davis.

When I arrived in New Orleans, I learned that to bet on Morrison you could get seven to five, but if you wanted Davis you had to lay eight to five. A bellboy at the quondam Hotel St. Charles said that things ought to pick up a bit, soon; with Davis in, the gaudy gambling halls in Jefferson Parish, just across the river, would be jumping again. Jefferson Parish proliferates with small places, but these, having a sordid aspect suggestive of chicanery, have little appeal for hotel guests. The big places needed a guaranteed immunity from state police interference to justify their high overhead. I have been for several years a satisfied subscriber to the Las Vegas, Nevada, *Sun,* and I knew the bellboy's view was shared out there.

Paul McIlheny, a faithful Morrison man I met in the hotel lobby, said he was going down to Iberia Parish, where he lives, to vote and shoot a deer on Saturday and would not come back to New Orleans to listen to election returns in Morrison headquarters.

Next morning I called a Louisiana elder statesman, and he said, "Chep has run rings around Davis in the campaign, but the logistics are against him. In the first primary, it was one city Catholic boy against four Protestant country boys. Now there's just one of them. It's a shame."

Morrison, I read in the paper, was still full of fight.

He said: "The most shocking fact of the campaign is that the newspapers who have almost universally stood for what is right and proper have thrown their arms around the combination of Davis and Long."

For the hell of it I telephoned John F. Tims, president of the *Times-Picayune* Company, to ask him why they had dumped Morrison, but Mr. Tims, while courteous, sounded testy. (He did not ask me to run around to his office and share a jambalaya.) He said they just liked Davis better. Morrison, he admitted, had "made a reasonably good Mayor." I could have asked a number of rhetorical questions, but they would have come under the head of twitting, so I said goodbye.

It was clear that Tims was not afraid of lining Louisiana up with the grass-eating states like Mississippi, nor ashamed of Rainach and Comiskey, so long as the *Times-Picayune* could say it had elected a governor. There was still less use asking him if it didn't feel silly to take a swing at Earl and wind up with Earl in his whiskers. He bought the shoes to fit hisself.

It was the result of the primary election that was to steel the Negro college students' hearts for the April demonstrations in New Orleans and Baton Rouge. They knew by then that gradualism was no good.

I dressed and went down to breakfast, regretting, as I walked the worn old zodiac carpet, that after the election I might not have a reasonable excuse to return to New Orleans for a long time. I could not think of anything more useful to do that afternoon than to go to the races at the Fair Grounds.

But Tom, who is a more thorough reporter than I, joined me in the coffee room and said there was something I must see before I left, in order to understand what I meant to write about: a white-on-white, like a gambler's shirt, bleached-in-the-bone, like a dead camel, segregationist of superior social standing. (It is an affront to speak of a "dyed-in-the-wool" segregationist, because "wool" suggests African origin.)

Tom is obsessed with the South, and particularly with his littoral, where he was born. He went North once, in about 1940, as a Nieman fellow at Harvard and became an editor of *The New Republic,* but New Orleans drew him back before he could get it in perspective.

It is one more city of the Graecia Maxima that rims the Mediterranean, and the professionally reputable New Orleans surgeon he took me to see was the counterpart of the anti-Semitic doctor I had visited in Oran in 1942. Both were white-haired and clean and suggested dowagers; both were amiably amused at their visitors' "ignorance" of "basic truths" about history (and ethnology, sociology, economics) although withholding blame, because a world conspiracy of educators worked against truth.

Both had an inverted understanding of all these subjects, like a Mennonite's of geography or an astrologer's of causation. They were initiates, objective and without rancor. The man in Oran said he rather liked Jews, personally, although it was a taste that, regrettably, few others shared, since ritual murder, a well-attested practice, put people off, as did Jews' lascivious character and general complicity in a world conspiracy of bankers and Bolshevists. My New Orleans surgeon said that *he* liked Negroes, or at least the good old ones he had known in Clinton, Louisiana, when he was a boy, who took in good part the Divine limitation of their intelligence.

"Allow me to read you a line or two from this book that illustrates," he said, pulling from a stack a foot high a copy of a pamphlet that he later gave me: "God Laughs at the Race-Mixers, 101 best jokes on Mixiecrats versus Dixiecrats," compiled by Rev. Carey Daniel, Pastor, First Baptist Church of West Dallas, Southern Baptist Convention.

" 'We usually quit calling White men "boys" when they have passed their twenty-first birthday. But it is not at all uncommon to hear someone say, "Hey, boy," when address-ing some mature black man who may be up in his fifties or sixties. Mentally he is still an adolescent, and he doesn't feel the least bit offended by that implication—unless, of course, some white agitator has "done been talking to him." ' "

The doctor put the pamphlet down and folded his soft white hands over the gently rounded surgical smock. He leaned back in his swivel chair. "Good, isn't it?" he said. He picked up his Golden Treasury again and read another de-lightful spoof:

" 'A good old-fashioned coal-black Negro has summed it up in a nutshell: "It sho do look like some of them there *Ne-groes* is gonna get us niggers into a heap o' trouble." ' "

Having finished with the *amuse-gueules,* the doctor rubbed a hand over his profile—like a white-haired Robert Morley's—and then shoved the pamphlet over to me as a gift, to which he added others called "God the Original Segregationist," by the same Rev. Carey Daniel (who is the brother of the Governor of Texas) and "Which Way the Nation, Which

Way the South?" an address by the Rev. James P. Dees, Statesville, North Carolina, to the Citizens' Council of Greater New Orleans.

I still read them from time to time, whenever news from South Africa puzzles me.

"To revert to seriousness," the doctor said. "There are well-meaning people who object to the Supreme Court's interpretation of the Fourteenth Amendment, both as to voting rights and the Black Monday integration decision. The essential fact is that the Fourteenth Amendment does not exist. It was never legally enacted. *That* is the point that has never been debated before the Supreme Court yet—and when it *is,* the whole structure of tyranny imposed upon the South is going to fall, like a house of cards. The Fourteenth Amendment was imposed on the United States by one mulatto woman—Lydia Smith, the mistress of Thaddeus Stevens. To please her, Stevens forced it upon the prostrate body of the disfranchised South. *It was never legally ratified.*

"The so-called Legislature of the Southern States that under pressure ratified the three Reconstruction amendments did not represent the white people of the South. Let me clarify." And pulling out another pamphlet from the inexhaustible pile, he read, pausing frequently to wet his lips:

" 'Lying in separate graveyards in Lancaster, Pennsylvania, are the bones of Thaddeus Stevens and his mulatto mistress of many years, Lydia Smith.' "

"You see what kind of fella brought us into this situation," the doctor said jovially. "A hundred per cent integrationist." He resumed reading:

" 'Thin white bones they are now, deceptively still, as

inert, apparently, as the dust to which they are returning. Yet out of those graves there seeps to this day the vapor of a hatred so intense that it has lived to curse our nation for nearly a hundred years.'

"Lydia started it all," the doctor said. "I'll be glad to give you the book, to peruse at your leisure. Now I'll just skip to the end, to give you the essence of it."

He read again:

" 'The conspirators'—that's Thad and Lydia—'realized that a Constitutional Amendment would be necessary to supersede States' Rights and override forever the objection of either individuals or State Legislatures. Stevens admitted to Lydia that because of the manner of its adoption, the Fourteenth would not be constitutional, and it is recorded that he admitted as much to several Senators as cynical as himself.'

"And they got away with it," the doctor said. "I'll just leave you with the author's conclusion and then let you have the book:

" 'On July 28th, 1869, when the sticky Washington summer was at its height, the Fourteenth Amendment, bastard child of Lydia and Stevens, became the law of the land.

" 'At that moment Stevens' mind blacked out forever. He knew he had revenged his Lydia. Life smoldered fitfully within his frame for two weeks longer, but consciousness was gone. He had died in the full knowledge that his curse upon the South could spread like a black stain until it engulfed the entire country. . . .

" 'In view of the evidence gathered from history, we submit that in no single way can the Fourteenth be regarded as constitutional. Pull down the Fourteenth, even as Samson split open the supporting pillars, and the whole structure of intolerable laws, based upon it'—He has laws in parentheses," the doctor said, with a chuckle—" 'will dissolve into the dust.' " He put the pamphlet down and looked at me with friendly superiority.

"You're supposed to be an educated man," he said, "and I'll wager you never knew that before."

I confessed I hadn't, and that it put the matter in an entirely new light for me. I had always thought of the Fourteenth as a defense of liberties rather than a violation: "No State shall make or enforce any law which shall abridge the privileges or immunities of citizens of the United States . . ." and the rest of it.

"But to be realistic," I said, "do you think there's a chance that in any near future you could get Congress and three quarters of the states to repeal it? And what can you do in the meanwhile?"

The doctor said that one thing Jimmie Davis could do, if the United States Court ordered the New Orleans School Board to open the way to race mixing by admitting a Negro to a white school, was to enjoin the School Board from complying. A peculiarity of the cult is that they all believe Negroes sexually irresistible. "He could put the Board members in jail, if they didn't comply with his injunction," the doctor said. "He has promised to do that, if the occasion arises, even if he has to go to Federal prison himself."

That night, another segregationist, a Mr. Emil Wagner, speaking from a New Orleans television station, made the same promise, in the candidate's name. Governor Davis had assured him he would go to jail for the Cause, if necessary, Wagner said.

I added the historical pamphlet—Lydia Smith and the Fourteenth Amendment—to the bundle and thanked the good physician, who said it was nothing at all, he was always glad to help a Northerner understand the South.

"You can't always believe what you read in the press," he said with a chuckle. "Did you know that after the War Between the States, when the Yankee newspapers were trying to stir up hard feelings about the Ku Klux Klan, Yankee correspondents used to come down here and dress up in white sheets and go out and kill niggers to stir up excitement? It's all in that book. Now don't you go killing any. Ha, ha."

When we got outside and I saw the palm trees in the front yards, I said to Sancton that it was all just like Oran, but he said the resemblance was superficial.

I said we weren't going to waste the morrow in any such fashion as we had today. Come hell or high water, we would go out to the races. That evening by luck we met Glen Douthitt, one of Morrison's staff, outside Kolb's German restaurant on St. Charles Avenue, and when we said we were going racing he gave us two seats in the Mayor's box, which is one away from the Governor's over the finish line. In Kolb's they serve planked redfish steak, snapping-turtle fricassee, jambalaya and gumbo, as well as pig's knuckles and wursts, so that their diapason is wider than a German restaurant's in less favored regions. The cuisine has undergone a sea change, like that Alsatian joint's in Tunis.

Kolb's is noisy and as full of politicians as rye bread of caraway seeds. At dinner, Tom and I met another elder statesman, who said there had been only one true thing said in the whole campaign: "And that was when Chep Morrison said he would do anything to win. But he took it back."

Next morning I awoke cheerful, because I was going racing. The *Times-Picayune*'s front page reflected a lip-licking calm. Davis predicted a victory by from 75,000 to 150,000 in the state. A Mr. Wogan, Morrison's campaign manager in New Orleans, predicted Morrison would win by 115,000 in the city and then sweep on to take upstate again, but this was obviously a dream—there were only 200,000 voters registered, and positing a 90 per cent vote, which was high, the Mayor would have to beat Davis *and* the RDO by a margin of 5 to 1, to live up to Wogan.

In the event, Morrison beat Davis by 33,000 votes in New Orleans, 103,000 to 70,000. This was a fairly notable performance. In 1956, against Earl Long, who, like Davis, had the aid of the Regular Democratic Organization, Morrison had had the dithyrambic endorsement of the *Times Picayune* *and* the then breathing *Item,* and even with the newspapers dancing before him like priests of Adonis had won by only 2,000 votes. With the *Times-Picayune*'s aid, or even neutrality, this time—if it be supposed that a monopoly newspaper influences even 10 per cent of its captive audience—Morrison would have beaten Davis in the city by 120,000 votes to 53,000.

As I lay abed in the old St. Charles, in the sunlight of a cold, clear day, I could not help ruminating, with the delight of the contemplative, on how many changes in the sand-whirl politics of the westernmost Arab state I had witnessed since I had arrived, in late summer, to report on Earl Long's mad-

ness. Nobody talked of that any more, least of all the doctors
who had predicted his instant disintegration. I remembered
with pleasure a report I had read in the *Times-Picayune* of
a manifesto put out by some psychiatrists in North Carolina,
protesting because old Earl had fired the doctors who said he
was crazy and replaced them by doctors who said he wasn't.
Doctors, like publishers, detest insubordination.

(My own amateur diagnosis had been that all he needed
to calm him down was a square meal of fried steak, grits,
busters, pompano, guinea hen, country ham and watermelon, and a case of 10-cent beer, and then perhaps twenty-
four hours to digest it.)

When I arrived, Earl, with only Jim Comiskey and the Old
Regulars to help him, had been the betting favorite for Governor. Lined up against him had been Morrison the reformer,
Rainach the grass-eater, and Peace-and-Harmony Davis, with
the *Times-Picayune* assumed to be for Morrison because of
its pious past.

Subverting Comiskey, the rest had ganged up on Long,
and then, when he was out of the way, all but Morrison had
ganged up on Morrison. Lastly they had had to invite the
Imam in again, and now all were dancing in a ring, old Earl
holding hands in turn with Comiskey, who had held his hand
before, with the *Times-Picayune,* the enemy of the Longs and
Comiskey forever, with Willie Rainach, who had been his
opponent in debate when the Governor blew his top defend-
ing Negro rights, and with Davis, the easiest of all for Earl to
understand.

The *Times-Picayune,* which had always been with Morrison against Long, was now with Long against Morrison. It

was like that other oil region where at lunch time Nasser was with Ibn Saud against Hussein, and at cocktail time Hussein was with Ibn Saud against Nasser. And, like those other Arabs, these were good at their own style of street fighting. When I came down to the street, I bought an early edition of the *States-Item* that carried a glaring front-page story:

NAB ARMED DEPUTY AT POLLS

which began:

A Negro deputy sheriff serving as a poll watcher was arrested this morning and booked with carrying a concealed weapon.

Felix McElroy, Sr., an official watcher for gubernatorial candidate Mayor Chep Morrison, was arrested shortly after 7 A.M. at the polling place of the 15th precinct of the Twelfth Ward, 2600 Peniston.

Frank Manning, chief investigator for the Attorney General's office and a support of former Governor Jimmie Davis for Governor, made the arrest.

Gun, Blackjack

Manning charged McElroy, wearing a gun and carrying a blackjack in his hip pocket, was "walking around polls in a manner which was intimidating to voters." *McElroy was wearing a Morrison lapel badge.* [my italics]

Manning disarmed McElroy and turned him over to Police Sgt. Jules Michel, who booked the deputy at Second District.

Michel said McElroy *was not intimidating voters or threatening them* [mine again], but was carrying a sidearm and blackjack partially visible under his jacket. . . .

McElroy was booked at 8 A.M. and paroled by Criminal District Judge Shirley G. Wimberley at 8.50 A.M.

The story of the armed Negro with the Morrison badge intimidating voters although the cop said he wasn't was a neat clincher to the Morrison-nigger axis stories put out throughout the campaign. The "investigator" who made the arrest was a Davis worker. The story disappeared inside the newspaper after the polls closed at 7 P.M., when it lost its news importance.

By that time Tom and I were back from the races and thinking of dinner, and when we had finished that, toward ten, word was already around town that the favorite was in.

In the first primary the Davis people had waited in vain for the count from upcountry to wipe out the Morrison lead. This time, though, the ratio of the Davis lead in the early returns from upstate to the Morrison majorities in New Orleans and the southern parishes pointed an ineluctable finger.

"Looks as if the town will open up, man," the lean old news vendor who sold me an early *Times-Picayune* at Royal and Canal said brightly. (Out in Las Vegas, the *Sun* headlines said: "Election of Davis Big Victory for Gamblers—New Governor Promises 'Normalcy' in Louisiana.") That was fine with me; I like roulette in a clean, well-lighted place.

"Within four years, Rainach be Governor," I heard a cab driver with a redneck accent say to the talker in front of a strip-tease bar.

We walked about the old town, getting the results piece-meal on radios in different bars. It wasn't a great victory, but the consortium candidate ate into Morrison's early lead steadily.

When Davis went ahead, we were in a new place Pete

Herman had opened on Bourbon Street. Pete wasn't at ease in the new place because he couldn't remember his way around. Watching him in the old one, where he had been for thirty-five years, you would have trouble telling he was blind. (He has gone back since, and he's all right.) Pete had no radio going in his joint because the sound would have clashed with the strip-tease music. So he got the returns by telephone; I don't know who was at the other end, but they kept coming.

Pete would put down the phone and say, "Morrison only leading by eight thousand now," and next time, "Davis is still coming on," as if it were a fight. He could tell by the music what stripper was on the stage, and he would say, "That's a sweet kid," or "She got quite a novelty there." Sometimes there would be a busload of tourists in the joint, and sometimes the three of us would be sitting alone.

The strippers went right on, even when there was no one there. He talked about infighting, his great art, but he made it sound simple, as if Daumier had said to you, "All there is to it is drawing." "All you want," Pete said, "is get that left hand under your arm, and keep hitting. You don't want to hold, do you? What good does that do you? Keep hitting."

The bull shoulders twitched with a remembered pleasure.

The phone clicked, and he picked it up again. When he put it down he said, "Davis goes ahead three thousand."

We walked over to Morrison headquarters as we had on the first primary night a month earlier. Symptomatically, even the locus had changed. The Morrison people had lost their lucky election-night suite at the Sheraton-Charles, because it had been reserved months earlier for some convention.

They were at the Jung, a less famous hotel, on Canal Street, and when we got there hope had already fled.

Some of the women workers were in tears. There were only petits-fours and empty bottles left on the buffets. Television operatives were all over the place, and there were a couple of depressed reporters. Reporters usually root against their employers, and they are distressed when their paper has a winner. With nearly all the state's precincts in, Davis had it by 70,000 votes—about 480,000 to 410,000.

The television people were waiting for the Mayor to concede, a gruesome ritual of the profession in which the loser is led before the cameras like the leading character in a lynching. And, like the prospective lynchee, he is expected to show spunk. The Mayor did, thanking all the people who had worked for him and pretending that he did not feel terrible.

One of the politicos told me that Earl Long had already been on the phone to Camille Gravel, bragging on having pulled Davis through. He claimed all the credit. He said Davis had been well licked when he pitched in and saved him. Morrison had carried Jefferson, the dormitory parish across the river, where the householders were not as happy as the parish officials about the return of big gambling. He had run well in southern, Hellenistic, littoral Louisiana, with the exception of Plaquemines, where Perez, holding his votes until he saw how many would be needed, had checked in late with a three-to-one majority for Davis. (If the contest had still looked close, the boss might have bettered that.) But the north, the region in which only Earl could have cut into the Davis vote, had gone completely, lopsidedly Protestant country boy-White League.

"What Morrison needed," the politico added, alluding to the Davis songbook, "was 35,000 less Baptists in the state and 35,000 more high-stepping browns."

As for Uncle Earl, in whose welfare I had begun to take a deep interest in the days when I first realized that he was the only effective Civil Rights man in the South, he was doing fine when I last saw him.

Out at the Fair Grounds that afternoon, I had lost three straight ten-dollar bets sitting in the box that poor Morrison was too worried about other matters to be in, when, happening to turn to my right, I saw a wide, healthy, sun-reddened hog-hunter's face grinning at me from under a wide, parsnip-colored hat.

It was the fine Governor, and would be until his term ended in May, of the Great State of Louisiana. His work was done, and he had nothing to worry about—it wasn't his election. A commissionaire had just brought him a couple of fresh handfuls of hundred-dollar bills. The system he had declined to tell me about was evidently working, and he appeared to be up to the weight he had been before he started dieting and got into all that trouble.

Later I was to read a speech he made at the State Labor Convention in which he said, "Don't you sell old Uncle Earl short—there's a lot of good reading in old books."

As he stuffed all that money in his pocket, another stout, jolly, ruddy man, also a winner, strolled over to his box and leaned over the edge, and they had a good laugh together. It was Jimmy Noe, who had endorsed Morrison, and the two companions of the Prophet looked as happy and well-attuned

as Laurel and Hardy, except they looked more like two
W. C. Fieldses.

I hate to bother a man about Louisiana politics when he is
engaged in a serious occupation like handicapping, so I just
waved to him. Earl looked to me like one of the sanest horse-
players I have seen in years. I once knew a psychiatrist who
played "best bets" supplied him by three nationally advertised touts every day and hardly ever collected a dime.

CHAPTER **XV**

THE LAST RACE

If the race meeting at the Fair Grounds had not ended, as it always does, in early spring, Earl Long might be with us today. Continuing in the salubrious pursuit of overlays and sleepers, he would have stoked the glow of health in his cheeks by day and relaxed his arteries in the company of squirmers in the evening. A squirmer is a strip-teaser who, having exhausted the possibilities of the vertical, exercises her art horizontally, recumbent on a chaise longue above the back bar with its array of spuriously labeled liquor bottles. Prone, she produces alternate clockwise and counterclockwise ventral vibrations, synchronized with opposed mammary rotations and what she conceives to be a facial reflection of extreme passion. With her legs, meanwhile, she performs a calisthenic of easily penetrable symbolism.

Between squirms, as presented in New Orleans, there are long intervals designed to induce the customers to leave, making place for newcomers who will pay the minimum cover charge of two and a half dollars for a drink. Nobody in his right mind ever takes a second. During the intervals the girls have time for long abstract conversations with their friends. The fine Governor, a lively lame duck, enjoyed these dialogues. They took his mind off politics. He averred that his interest in the squirmers was strictly avuncular.

Under Louisiana law he had four months in which to get his things together before leaving the State House. The theory behind the hiatus is either that a Governor of Louisiana must have accumulated during his term of office at least twice as much loot as a President of the United States, who has only two months in which to clear out after *his* successor's election, or that he must be twice as tired. This should have been a period of continued recuperation for Earl. His system had been subjected to a strain that would have mashed a Marciano to the ground.

To have been forcibly dislodged from the executive mansion, like a limpet from an oyster shell, and then to have waked in a madhouse, ticketed insane, is about as near nightmare as a man in his senses can come. The long struggle back to freedom must have taken a lot more out of him, and he had followed that with six months of uninterrupted campaigning, of the sort I had witnessed in Alexandria in the summer of 1959. Each of us has a threshold of endurance, and his was much higher than most men's. But there are limits.

The closing of the horse track interrupted the healthy regime, and he began to think of politics again. Some men carry in the backs of their minds the names of books they mean to

read when they have time. Earl carried grudges to get around
to. In 1958 his elder brother George, an ex-dentist, had been
Congressman from the Eighth District of Louisiana, which
includes Winnfield. The dentist died, and the fine Governor
supported an old friend and campaign contributor, a man
named Teekell, for nomination-election to fill the vacancy.
He considered the nomination within the family gift. But
the Eighth also includes Alexandria, and a man named
Harold B. McSween out of there beat Teekell in the primary.
Behind McSween was Camille Gravel, up to that moment a
trusted Long man. That was when Long and Gravel split.

Now, free of office, Uncle Earl determined to get even with
Representative McSween and, through him, get evener with
Gravel, whom he had already hurt through Morrison. He
entered the 1960 congressional primary in the Eighth District. (Congressional primaries are not held at the same time
with gubernatorial primaries in Louisiana, even when they
fall in the same year. Politicians in the Great State believe in
staggering their pleasures so there will be no closed seasons.)
In the first primary, with a mixed bag of candidates, Mc-
Sween topped the list by a couple of thousand votes, with
Uncle Earl a good second. The two candidates then made
their customary deals with the losers and them that had voted
for them. At this kind of retail dickering Earl was a master.

It was a mastery particularly helpful on the scale of a
congressional election. The second primary was set for August 27. I had a letter from Margaret Dixon dated August
22 that said Earl was "running up a storm" and likely to be
elected. I was in Rome for the Olympic Games, and would

have thought the weather there hot if I hadn't experienced Louisiana in the previous summer. But I could imagine the old man speaking from a truck at the crossroads in the villages with funny names: "I'm the best friend the poor white man, and the middle-class white man, and the rich white man, so long he behave himself, and the poor colored man, ever had." Probably six or eight speeches a day, and six or eight bottles of Coca-Cola used as ice cologne.

He beat McSween in the runoff by about 4,000 votes. That ended a tumultuous fifteen months beginning with his own exportation to the nuthouse.

Earl went into a hospital at Alexandria on the night after his victory, complaining that he had eaten a piece of bad pork at a barbecue. In fact, he had had a heart attack the night before the primary election, but would not admit it because it might have deterred people from voting for him. It reminded me of Pete Herman not letting Midget Smith know he was blind. Instead of going to the hospital when he had the attack, Earl had spent the primary day gasping with pain on his bed in the Hotel Bentley, that monument to municipal over-optimism where we all had spent the night after his 1959 speech in the courthouse square. He didn't allow himself to be taken to the hospital until after the polls had closed and the news couldn't hurt his chances.

Earl would have been a great addition to Congress, where nobody of his stature has sat since John Quincy Adams and John Morrissey, but he shifted the field of his activities in another direction. On September 5 he died.

A man he had staying with him for company at the hospital, one of the succession of driver-handyman confidants Earl always had about him, said, "He just drank a cup of coffee and went."

Like Hannibal, who lives in history only through the accounts of his enemies, Uncle Earl had to depend on a hostile press to write his obit. But the *Times-Picayune* and its afternoon caudal appendage and the press associations did him proud. Most reporters had liked Earl, and even those who didn't had the pride in him that a groom has in being associated with a "big horse." Their feelings showed in their stories, now that they were too late to do him any good.

Robert Wagner in the *Times-Picayune* implicitly recognized Earl's status as an Imam when he recorded that followers "greeted his death almost with disbelief."

"With single-minded tenacity, Long ran for Congress, despite warnings that he couldn't win. . . .

"He out-campaigned McSween, used hillbilly singing, free groceries, hams and watermelons to lure out the voters. But the rigors of the campaign were apparently too much for the seemingly indestructible Long. . . .

"Some Longites felt he had been more resigned to 'meeting my Maker' after vindicating himself, in his own mind, by defeating McSween."

Camille Gravel, quoted by the Associated Press, said the death "closes the amazing career of the most aggressive, determined and resourceful man of politics ever known to Louisiana and perhaps in any other state. I regret his passing."

Theo Cangelosi, the L.S.U. supervisor Long had called a special session of the Legislature to get rid of, said, "Earl possessed more raw courage and determination than any man I ever knew or read about." And he said Earl had a stronger personality than Huey. He said that when Huey wanted to resign during the impeachment fight, long ago, Earl made him stay in there and fight it out.

James McLean of the A.P., who covered the fine Governor for a long time, said, "Earl just didn't organize, and the reason was, said politicians who obeyed him, he never believed in letting two fellows in the camp know the same thing at the same time.

" 'He was psychic,' insisted Ed Coco of Marksville, one-time state director of registration and staunch Long colleague. He played a harmonica for campaign crowds in Long's recent Congressional fight. . . .

"In Coco's words, 'Earl was closer to the ordinary people than Huey. Earl really knew the poor people, the little people. He'd go back in the woods to shake hands with them, white or Negro.'

"If Long had reached the Congress, Coco said, 'he'd have exposed a lot of secrets. He believed in breaking up political nests. He just loved to do it.' "

A State Senator called Rayburn told McLean: "Long was a jovial kind of fellow, for us who knew him, with a heart bigger than most people will ever know. Long could have been selfish in some of his motives, but he would go out of his way to help a person in need. And he was a man not afraid of anything."

"David Bell, a 47-year-old cousin, . . . said, 'Earl always was a head-and-head politician. Give him 20 minutes with a local leader and he could almost sell any idea. Huey appealed through oratory and organization. . . .

" 'Earl must have died happy,' Bell insisted, 'because he died after doing what he loved best—politicking.'

"Dr. Felton Clark, president of Southern University, the largest land-grant Negro University in the South, said the three-time Governor, 'within the framework of his political outlook and philosophy, showed an active sympathy for the education of Negro people.

" 'He did so in big and little things, and with blunt, sudden speed,' the university president said. . . .

"The tale is told how a disgruntled supporter said he would look for Long with a .38-calibre pistol.

"Long, hearing this, so it is told, roared, 'Mr. Smith and Wesson makes them .38's all the same size.' . . .

"The stories about Long are endless."

Editorially the two kernels in the Tims peanut were less affectionate, but they had the tone I would expect of Billy Graham if he heard a reliable report of the demise of the Devil. They had nothing left to oppose except the Supreme Court of the United States.

Hardly had Earl's head fallen back upon the pillow when the onset of the mourners began, led by Miz Blanche, his widow, who said they had made up before he died, and United States Senator Russell B. Long, his nephew. Involuntarily, I remembered the fine Governor at Baton Rouge: "But the plane flew on to Galveston, and my sweet little wife hasn't showed up yet, neither my little nephew."

But it was a moment of general forgiveness. Representative Herbert B. McSween, whom Earl had just beaten out of his seat, was quoted saying, "His death, coming as it did, is a terrible shock to the district."

Earl's lying in state at Baton Rouge, whither he had been transported from Alexandria for the last time, with the state troopers' sirens blaring in front of him as always as the cortege clipped along at fifty miles an hour, was incessantly interrupted by the necessity of changing the blankets of flowers over his casket. Friends and ex-enemies had sent them by the gross, and whoever it was that ran the funeral felt they should all have a showing. He started under a blanket of white chrysanthemums sent by Huey's widow, who was in Colorado, and finished under white and violet orchids presented by some millionaire Longites who fell into temporary misfortune in the post-Huey scandals of 1940.

"The quantity of flowers, which had been meager early in the day, had mushroomed into a garden of flowers later in the evening," Wagner wrote.

All day long viewers passed the coffin at the rate of ten a minute—most of them, but not all, Long people like the taxi driver I had talked to in Baton Rouge and the old man in the crowd on the courthouse lawn. The *Times-Picayune* reported, "An unexpected visitor was Blaze Starr, showgirl friend of Long." (I expect Long would have expected her, though; she had been on his side when a lot of the political mourners weren't.) "She arrived with a sister, Debbie, and two friends, Jose Martinez, manager of the Bourbon St. 'Sho-Bar,' and Polly Kavanaugh, worker at the bar."

The *Times-Picayune* I saw printed a poem by a Mrs. Delma

Harrell Abadie of Donaldsonville, written "while en route here on a bus." I venture to reproduce it:

> The farmer-politician is gone, oblivious to friend and foe,
> You can't say he was a quiet man, for he talked with force,
>   long and loud,
> And whether it was his words or actions, he always drew and
>   held a crowd.

It is a requiem that I think Uncle Earl would have liked.

CHAPTER XVI

LA. WITHOUT EARL

Last summer, while Earl was still slugging it out at the cross-roads with McSween, I had a letter from a man in Louisiana consisting mostly of a copy of the following United Press International dispatch published in the *States-Item* of August 6:

> BATON ROUGE (UP)—The newly-formed state welfare board yesterday approved a welfare spending cutback of $7,640,000 this year, made possible by a purge of illegitimate children from assistance rolls.
>
> After electing Alexandria banker James Bolton its chairman the board heard a report that 22,650 children have been struck from the state aid rosters because they live in common-law marriage homes or because their mothers bore illegitimate children after taking state aid.
>
> The purge was responsible for a cut of $6,300,000 in state aid [the Federal Government's contribution to the support of these children] federal funds. The children are dependents of 6,014 families.

The report was presented by assistant administrator O. C. Sills who said about 90 percent of the children taken from the rolls were Negroes.

My correspondent added:

"The above is a result of legislation passed by the Jimmie Davis legislature disfranchising people of bad moral reputation.

"Perhaps you should come back and do a profile on Jimmie Davis."

The net saving to the state of Louisiana, I calculated from this dispatch, would be $1,340,000—a handsome return for starving 22,000 children to death. It works out, roughly, to a saving of $61 on each small victim. If the state withholds its portion of the funds it automatically blocks off the Federal contribution, too, because Congress has set a fixed ratio of Federal to state aid. With each $61 of savings, the grass-eaters running the state under Davis thus got as a free bonus another $244 worth of revenge on a child for being colored.

Remembering Earl's great appeal to the Legislature, I wondered how many of the fathers were white.

In retrospect the fine Governor ("Niggers are human beings"; "Lincoln was right") seemed more than ever the most effective liberal in the South. While he was in office he had barred this kind of thing. The action seemed so atrocious, however, that I surmised something—perhaps a protest by the now remorseful, repentant *Picayune*—would occur at the last moment to stop it from happening.

Louisiana was only occasionally on my mind while I was in Rome, and the only tidings I had from there came in occasional notes. But on Sunday, September 11, while reading a copy of *The Observer,* of London, which reaches Rome by air on the date of publication, I came upon the following story, which moved the Great State minus Earl into almost the international prominence of the Union of South Africa.

Chep Morrison had long made conscientious efforts to direct international attention upon the city of New Orleans, but the results were puny compared to what the new regime had achieved:

Louisiana Shocked by British Offer

Help for Starving Negroes

From GEORGE SHERMAN

NEW ORLEANS, Louisiana, September 10. Racial prejudice and the complicated machinery of welfare administration in the United States are frustrating efforts to save 6,000 unmarried mothers and 23,000 children from starvation in Louisiana.

Ninety-five per cent of these people are Negroes. They were struck from the State welfare rolls at the end of July, when Governor Jimmie Davis—armed with a new State law —ruled that public money could no longer support "immoral" women who had illegitimate children.

A letter in a local newspaper expresses the prevalent sentiment among whites: "It is doing an injustice to the people to place this burden of taxation on our shoulders; it is encouraging a great evil and is a disgrace to this State."

But there are some small signs that the white public is beginning to realise that more is at stake here than local politics. News of national and international protest is filtering through. Critics are saying that the final result will be a boomerang against the strongly segregationist Governor.

Morning newspaper readers were shocked when they read a front-page dispatch from Newcastle-upon-Tyne saying that 15 women members of the city council had begun a campaign to send the "starving and illegitimate" Negro children to England.

Athlete's Return

Up to that point the local Press had relegated reports of misery and pleas for help to small items on inside pages. Money has come from Britain to help the children and more is on the way.

The tension between the races has all but destroyed whatever easygoing relationship existed. The bitter fight over integration of the schools and equal rights for the Negro has destroyed the middle ground of moderation for the time being at least.

The atmosphere to-day bears little resemblance to that in another Southern State, Tennessee, farther to the north, which is preparing to give a young Negress, Wilma "Skeeter" Rudolph, a welcome home from the Olympics in Rome, where she won three gold medals.

Supporters of Governor Davis's action in Louisiana admit that it is a punitive measure against Negroes. The new law itself is part of a "segregation package" passed in May in the State legislature. The parts of that package establishing a segregated school system under the Governor's direct control have subsequently been ruled unconstitutional. Schools in New Orleans will be integrated on November 14.

Prostitution Warning

Meanwhile implementation of the Welfare Act is having the effect intended. Negro leaders feel the State is showing how "tough" it can be if they persist in their efforts at integration. The door has been opened for removing "immoral" Negro women from voting rolls, as well as welfare rolls. And this spotlight on the high rate of illegitimacy among Negroes has effectively reinforced fears of the white people about "mixing" their children in integrated schools.

The practical result has been a flight of desperate mothers to the private welfare agencies. The hardest hit is the bi-racial Urban League of Greater New Orleans. Seven hundred women have appealed to the league in the past two weeks. "In the mood these people are in they will do anything for food. The rate of prostitution is bound to rise," said a young white social worker.

Representatives of the dozen most powerful white and Negro social and Church organizations in New Orleans have announced that they cannot cope. They estimate that 5,000 children in New Orleans alone are nearing starvation.

Funds Run Out

"The question is no longer integration versus segregation, white versus Negro, State responsibility versus Federal responsibility; it is a question of feeding hungry children," said Mr. Revius Ortique, president of the Urban League. He, like the other spokesmen, did not condone immorality, but said the law was punishing children for the sins of their parents.

Mr. Ortique said the Urban League had had to close its emergency food dispensing headquarters. Funds had run out. The Rev. A. W. Ricks, Negro representative of the New Orleans Council of Methodists, said he had turned his church into a relief centre for 36 families, but he could no longer find the necessary money to support them.

Father Ray Hebert, Director of Associated Catholic Chari-
ties, said no single private agency could handle the demand.
Children in Catholic parishes throughout the city were
begging for food. Some were rummaging in garbage bins.

Federal Intervention

Seventy-five per cent. of the $29 million annually spent in
Louisiana on dependent children comes from the Federal
Government in Washington. The State is really the administrator of national funds. To qualify, it must conform to a
national code of rules laid down in the Federal Social Se-
curity System. State welfare workers here say that Federal
intervention is the chief hope for saving the situation.

According to Federal rules, illegitimacy *per se* is not
ground for refusing relief. The unmarried mother, like the
married mother, must prove that she maintains a "suitable
home." The Louisiana legislature has simply made illegitimacy one proof of an "unsuitable home."

The Federal Government has taken the first step towards
cutting off Louisiana funds. The Department of Health,
Education and Welfare wrote to State welfare authorities
voicing concern over the dropping of the 6,000 cases in one
month. All Federal money is to be stopped, unless the State
can provide some evidence that illegitimacy has not been
made the sole criterion for determining the suitability of the
home.

I am not one of those Americans who think we should
pattern our way of life—the Southern way of life, the Northern way of life, the Western way of life, or the Eastern, North-
eastern, Northwestern, Southeastern or Southwestern ways
of life, or for that matter the Hawaiian or Alaskan ways of

life—primarily to win the approval of a lot of piffling foreigners. I therefore discounted the *Observer*'s story as an example of that precious British sentimentality that led British humanitarians to invade the Soviet Embassy in London in 1957 to protest against putting dogs in rockets. Many unmarried mothers try, illegally, to get rid of their children before they are born, and letting them starve to death is a time-tested and, in Louisiana now, a state-sanctioned method of getting rid of them as soon after they are born as possible. It is better than abortion because it saves the mothers from committing a Mortal Sin, and better than letting the children live because they would then grow up in unsuitable surroundings and some might eventually become members of the NAACP. The Louisiana law is a promising demographic innovation in the Western world, and I was amazed, shortly after my return to these shores, to read an editorial in the New York *Times* that, in slavish imitation of the meddling foreigner, denounced it.

The Longs, Earl and Huey before him, blocked such ameliorations of the Southern way of life in Louisiana, and whenever I read about the fine things the State Administration is doing down there now I remember the triumphant and original political cartoon in the *States-Item* after the first gubernatorial primary, which showed a tombstone with the inscription "Here Lies Longism."

In the *Herald-Tribune* of October 8, for example, I read a story that began: "New Orleans, Oct. 7 (UPI)—Louisiana Attorney General Jack Gremillion, who last summer bellowed that a Federal court was a 'den of iniquity,' today sobbed with joy when he was spared a jail sentence for criminal contempt of court.

"Federal District Judge Edwin F. Hunter said Mr. Gremillion was 'a fighter, and the world loves a fighter, but he fought out of bounds' when he called a three-judge integration suit panel a 'kangaroo court' Aug. 26. He sentenced Mr. Gremillion to eighteen months on his own good behavior.

" 'He told me I'm free,' the overjoyed Attorney General told reporters and well-wishers after adjournment. 'I'm very satisfied with the sentence and grateful to Judge Hunter for his fairness.' . . .

"Pleading for a light sentence, State Rep. Wellborn Jack likened Mr. Gremillion to 'the manager of a ball team which hasn't won a game in six years' [a figure of speech for the segregationists in the Federal Courts]. He said such a losing streak would cause any one to lose his head 'in the heat of battle.' " It would also cause a bright manager to suspect he had a bad ball team.

This item, peculiarly enough, made me think of what Earl had once said about isms: "I'm not against anybody for . . . any ism he might believe in except nuttism, skingameism and Communism."

Longism may be dead with Earl, because the junior United States Senator is a toned-down, atypical Long, which is the equivalent of a Samson with a store haircut. He is also howling publicly about the Supreme Court's persecution of Louisiana, to head off grass-eater opposition in the Senatorial primaries by showing that his teeth are as green as any man's.

But nuttism is doing fine.

p.s.—November 18, 1960:

As I send this manuscript finally to the publisher, the grass-eaters and the nuts have taken over the streets of New Orleans, cheered on by the State Government the *Times-Picayune* helped elect.—A.J.L.